Lifelong Learning

THE PROFESSIONAL EDUCATION SERIES

Walter K. Beggs, *Editor*
Dean Emeritus
Teachers College
University of Nebraska

Royce H. Knapp, *Research Editor*
Regents Professor of Education
Teachers College
University of Nebraska

Lifelong Learning

by

ROGER HIEMSTRA

Professor of Adult and
Extension Education
Iowa State University

PROFESSIONAL EDUCATORS PUBLICATIONS, INC.
LINCOLN, NEBRASKA

Library of Congress Catalog Card No.: 76-7114

ISBN   0-88224-029-3

2596609

Contents

5

CHAPTER 1

Lifelong Learning: A Necessity

LIFELONG LEARNING FORCES

Societal interest in, and pressures for, lifelong learning are mounting. This new interest in education can be documented in many ways. Increasing adult and continuing education enrollments, a growing recognition of enormous educational deficiencies existing in the United States and other countries, mounting pressures for providing independent or non-traditional learning opportunities, and available evidence that formal school experience does not adequately equip people to cope with life's challenges are some major reasons cited in support of continuous learning needs. Later chapters and the various bibliographic references throughout this book provide more extensive documentation of the need for lifelong learning.

Three major forces have acted in concert to help create the interest in, and need for, lifelong learning. The first of these can be described simply as the rapidity and constancy of change. Societal change has been discussed and described in many ways by many people in recent years; therefore, an extended explanation is not needed in this chapter. However, there are some components of change that have had impact on the adult to specifically cause an increased need for learning.

Certainly Toffler and his renowned work related to the theme of *Future Shock* (see the Bibliography at the end of this chapter) has done as much as anyone else in focusing attention on the dangers of societal and technological change. Educators have started to realize that the life skills necessary to cope with rapid change, never-ending inflation, and constantly evolving lifestyles are not completely developed in formal K–12 schooling efforts. Thus, continuous change requires continuous learning. Unfortunately, there exist in society many adults unable or unwilling to change, to learn, or to manage their own lives satisfactorily—adults who frequently are led to believe that a better life awaits if only more and more of the material things produced by technological change can be obtained.

Illich has taken an even stronger stand through his revolutionary writings in which he suggests that immense inadequacies exist in formal schooling programs throughout the United States and other countries. He and others have suggested that normal schooling efforts and patterns are so designed that learners—especially the poor, the disadvantaged, and the ethnic minority—are inadequately prepared to cope with most of the main societal problems.

The results, they believe, are dysfunctionally schooled products who rely on further institutionalized education for problem solving rather than self-motivated learners who know how to avail themselves of a variety of resources, both personal and external, to cope with various problems.

A second major force, one certainly related to the first, is the continuous march by many adults toward occupational obsolescence. One way of describing this circumstance is to borrow from the nuclear physics field the concept of half-life. Occupational half-life is based on the assumption that enough new developments, techniques, and/or knowledge evolve in a short period of time, say 5–15 years, so that a person becomes roughly half as competent to do the job for which his or her initial training was intended. Consequently, adults frequently must turn to learning activities just to maintain or regain competence.

The third force that has helped create the interest in, and need for, lifelong learning deals with the change in lifestyles or value systems affecting so many people. Call it increased leisure, a movement toward self-actualization, or the "back-to-earth" interest, more and more people are believing that a full and rich life is possible primarily through the maximization of individual potentiality. Consequently, an increasing attention toward interpersonal communication skills, values clarification, and self-identity activities is becoming very recognizable in people's learning efforts.

These three forces have done much to heighten an awareness of adult and continuing education activities as viable means for obtaining necessary knowledge or skill. However, to enhance the development of people's potential, it is suggested that many of the basic attitudes and skills possessed by educators toward learners and the learning process must change. The idea of dispensing preestablished knowledge to a vacuum in the form of a student will need to be supplemented by, and in many instances exchanged for, a cooperative relationship between the learner and teacher in a mutual process of problem solving, self-discovery, and just plain learning how to learn.

INNOVATIVE APPROACHES TO THE EDUCATION OF ADULTS

Learning how to learn and how to solve problems through self-inquiry activities has not been easy for the adult student in traditional institutionalized courses or activities. More on the subject of the adult learner and learning styles will be contained in later chapters. However, it needs to be said here that many adults have resisted participating in, or after a short sampling have dropped out of, traditional learning activities. At the same time, various educational researchers have discovered that there exists much interest in learning by adults and an apparently high participation in learning endeavors outside normal institutional forms of education.

Consequently, education professionals have begun to pay particular attention to non-traditional forms for, and delivery systems of, learning. The following list represents some of the educational change taking place or about to take place in the American society:

Continuing Education Unit (CE U)—A new unit for measuring participation in a variety of formal and informal learning activities (ten classroom hours of instruction equals one CEU). In some instances, this unit replaces the college credit.

Learning modules—Short credit or noncredit blocks of learning in which a person can participate independently, as needed, at home, at work, or at community learning centers. Often the learner has an option of choosing from among several approaches, such as tape/slide kits, books, or films.

Credit for experience—The granting of college credit for community service, life experiences, or occupational experiences.

Credit by testing—The granting of a certain amount of credit, usually college credit, through an examination program. The College Proficiency Examination Program (CPEP) and the College-level Examination Programs (CLEP) are the most widely used systems.

Non-regular semester college offerings—The offering of mini-courses, internships, travel courses, and weekend courses for college credit.

External degree—Known also as the open-university or campus-without-walls approach, this usually refers to the granting of a college degree based on a variety of learning experiences, formal courses, and tutorially assisted activities, most of which take place outside of the traditional college campus.

Cable television—The use of television in the home, at work, or in neighborhood resource centers, often combined with some type of tutorial service, to present learning opportunities on a variety of topics.

Performance contracting—The mutual negotiation between an educational facilitator-expert and a learner on some specified learning activity with an agreed-upon level of performance to be obtained.

The adult learning project—A deliberate effort to learn something new, primarily through self-initiated efforts and typically outside of any institutionalized structure (more specific information on this topic will be contained in a later chapter).

Cassette instruction—The use of audio or video cassettes containing specific instruction or knowledge primarily for independent, individualized learning. Home-use video cassettes are a near-reality.

Voucher system for learning—Each person is entitled to a certain number of years of education but the education could be obtained any time in a lifetime that help was needed.

Open entrance/open exit—A person will be able to enter the school setting for a self-determined period of time and then exit, often with a plan for later reentry and study.

Universal bill of educational rights—A guarantee to every citizen of access to the widest possible educational opportunity. Related to the voucher system for learning, each person would probably be guaranteed some time off from a job for learning.

Facilitative self-training workshops—Retreat-like settings in which individuals are helped by resource specialists to experience self-growth through values clarification, Gestalt therapy, transactional analysis, transcendental meditation, or the like efforts.

Such non-traditional activities, alternative learning modes, or innovative educational changes are based primarily on the assumption that lifelong learning is a natural circumstance of life within which autonomous, self-directed learners participate according to their needs and interests. More change can be expected and must happen if education is to meet a goal of truly helping people with a lifetime of challenges.

IMPLICATIONS FOR TEACHER EDUCATION

Lifelong learning changes and forces have not been recognized very readily in colleges of education throughout the United States. Curriculum updating, for example, is frequently geared to content changes with new information; attention is seldom given to finding ways of incorporating curriculum with the challenges that occur throughout a lifetime. Teachers and administrators frequently are taught that the school is an island to which people come for a predetermined amount of time, rather than viewing the school as one resource in an educative environment.

There is also growing evidence that advanced learning credentials possessed by individuals do not automatically signal all is well in life. National achievement test scores are decreasing over time, numerous doctoral degree holders are unable to find meaningful work, and school systems have been sued by students who claim they have not received a viable education.

Another frustrating problem educators must face is the continuing and plaguing problem of school dropouts. In many schools throughout the United States, dropout rates are increasing; the eventual price such individuals must pay can be enormous. Added to this dilemma is the complaint by many teachers that today's student often has a poor attitude about school and learning.

It is suggested that school people must learn to think of themselves more as educators, instead of fairly narrow specialists such as high school science teachers, junior high counselors, or elementary school principals, if learning is to become lifelong instead of something that is discontinued at age 16, 18, or 22. Furthermore, the role of the teacher in a learning setting must change before such a suggestion can become a reality.

There are numerous views regarding the role of the teacher in a learning setting. Perhaps the most widely accepted view is that the teacher is one who imparts knowledge on a subject to others. Indeed, teacher training efforts frequently involve the development of content specialization by a teacher and, concurrently, the provision of training in various techniques, methods, and devices so that the person will become skillful in presenting any knowledge inherent in the specialization.

There are, however, potential weaknesses in the above-described training scheme, especially when adults are the students to be reached by teachers. First, if a receptor does not want to receive some predetermined knowledge because she or he is tired, fearful of the whole learning endeavor, or interested in something else—as can happen with adult learners of varying ages—then it is very difficult to simply impart some knowledge.

Second, a person receiving a piece of information incorporates that datum through his or her own eyes, knowledge limitations, and experience base. Thus, what a teacher might perceive as the important point on some topic might be perceived quite differently by the learner. Consequently, teacher education efforts must be aimed at more than the development of information transmittal skills.

As will be developed further in this and later chapters, the suggestion is made that teachers need to become more skilled as facilitators of, and resources in, the learning process. This will require that more attention be given to a discipline of learning where the rigor of analysis and the capacity to acquire new knowledge as needed are addressed foremost in the learning setting.

Such a role as facilitator and resource person includes one of helping learners determine their needs, discover what resources can be brought to bear on these needs, and match the resources with the needs. Learning in this type of arrangement becomes one of integrating the educational process with life's activities.

A point related to the one above is that in working with the student as an active partner in the educational process, each student has a potential, some need, and various experiences that will have a bearing on the teaching/ learning process. This factor moves the instructional process toward one of a cooperative student-teacher relationship, with the teacher as a facilitative resource person and the learner as an autonomous seeker of necessary knowledge. Such an ideal relationship is not obtained easily; however, it is something possible, particularly as both the learner and instructor become confident in the process.

As one leading adult and continuing educator characterized the type of arrangement being described thus far, the school, classroom, and community become learning resource centers and the teacher becomes a learning process consultant. In addition, this instructional approach will require the skills to promote self-inquiry, to involve students and others in program or course planning, and to facilitate individualized learning activities.

The discussion to this point has not meant to imply that lifelong learning needs have been totally unrecognized by teachers or teacher training institutions. Attempts to teach self-inquiry skills, individualization of instruction, team teaching, and the open classroom have all been efforts to improve learning attitudes and to develop useful learning skills. Indeed, it is expected that the movement toward creating lifelong learning skills will provide opportunities for teachers to improve or to shift their teaching styles and for colleges of education to do even better jobs.

Several needed changes related to teacher training are implied in the discussion above. First, if all teachers are to become effective in the facilitation of lifelong learning and in the utilization of a variety of innovative approaches to teaching or learning, they must come to grips with the concept of education as something broader than K–12 schools. The enclosure of education only within the institutional boundaries implied by a K–12 setting or even a K–college setting is not consistent with the constancy of needs emerging because of societal change. Thus, the expanding of educational abilities so that they foster continuous lifelong learning will require new commitments on the part of teachers in training, experienced teachers through in-service training, and teacher training institutions.

A second change suggested here is related to a pragmatic and economical need—teachers and educational administrators will need to be shown how better to make use of each community's total resources for education. Each teacher must learn how to use agency or individual expertise as supplemental and primary learning resources, how to help parents and children use community resources in solving problems, and how to develop curricula that help students understand the relationships between subject matter and later or emerging lives in the community. These changes will require that educators in training be exposed to community theory, be able to work closely with parents and community leaders, be exposed to the community through off-campus activities, and be involved in studying communities and their resources through community survey techniques. (More information on this theme will be presented in a later chapter.)

School administrators, support staff, college/university personnel, and even teachers themselves should also be prepared for active involvement in the community. There is a variety of community problems, such as the school dropout situation or the person unemployed because of skill obsolescence, that have a fairly direct connection to the educational scene; however, most of these problems are not being solved in any systematic fashion.

The third change involves helping each educator become skilled at facilitating education for people of all ages and backgrounds. In addition to general adult and youth groups that probably come quickly to mind, the following are suggested as special groups of people with educational needs:

Women—The consciousness-raising efforts of women's groups in recent years have uncovered a variety of continuing education needs and interests.
Elderly—Gerontology programs will become increasingly needed in the future.
Minority groups—Racial, ethnic, disadvantaged, and undereducated individuals have a multitude of needs not being met by traditional programs of education.

Health-related employees—The knowledge explosion has greatly affected health-related employees, especially those facing relicensure problems.

Citizen/consumer—Distrust of the political system, energy crises, continued inflation, and environmental concerns increasingly will prompt needs and interests related to consumer awareness and civic literacy.

Ways must also be discovered for meeting the educational needs of handicapped adults and people in correctional or other institutions. In addition, the entire area of job retraining will increasingly require the expertise of skilled educators.

Certainly those educators being prepared specifically for the adult education profession will work with the above groups as well as with programs designed to meet general adult interests and needs. However, because so many people who eventually work with educational programs for adults arrive in such positions by accident rather than by design and because this "Professional Education Series" is aimed foremost at K–12 teachers and lay persons, it is suggested that teacher preparation institutions—especially those that attempt to incorporate the concept of educator as a lifelong learning facilitator—need to consider the various types of clientele who will be recipients of educational efforts.

It is recognized that many implications of the changes suggested above cannot be accomplished overnight. Attitudes will need to change, innovations will need to be tried and tested, and new teaching strategies will need to be discovered. Hopefully, however, schools of education throughout the United States are beginning to meet such challenges with new and experimental approaches to their preparation efforts.

SOME PLAGUING PROBLEMS

There are several plaguing problems with which the educational profession must deal if lifelong learning is truly to become a reality. They will be enumerated here but not described in much specific detail. Educational philosophers, leaders, and practitioners will need to find the solutions.

1. Much greater precision is needed in defining what are inquiry skills or lifelong learning skills, what bearing, if any, age has on such skills, and how such skills might be taught.
2. In a lifelong learning environment, what will be the role of educational institutions and what will be the differences, if any, between techniques used by individuals working with children and those used in working with adults?
3. The concept of community (i.e., boundaries, roles, power structures, etc.) will require change to accommodate a lifelong learning environment.
4. How will the evolving teacher stance toward collective bargaining and striking affect the lifelong learning movement?
5. The related issues of financing education, needed legislation, and the rights of every citizen in the United States will need to be examined thoroughly.

6. The two or three generations of individuals caught between a traditional education structure and a lifelong learning society will need to be given special attention.
7. The role of higher education in a lifelong learning environment will need to be examined.

WHERE DO WE GO FROM HERE?

There is no magical way of summing up the thoughts made to this point nor of drawing any magnanimous conclusions upon which a new society built around lifelong learning can be created. As a matter of fact, much of the discussion offered thus far has not been very profound or new. However, it is suggested here that for whatever the reasons—bureaucratic or administrative hurdles, institutional handcuffing, or overworked/underpaid teachers—huge educational challenges remain. Furthermore, the intent of this chapter was not to provide a profound statement on societal ills, to attack the educational system in the United States, or to present a third-world view of a better life potential; rather, it was presented to provide a backdrop for the chapters to follow.

There are tremendous opportunities today and tomorrow in continuing education—both for professional continuing educators and those prepared primarily for work in K–12 schooling efforts—as it is predicted by many that adult and continuing education will be one of the few growth areas in education. However, such opportunities are dependent, for the most part, on lifelong learning becoming a reality for all. John Dewey stated it much better: "Education is not a preparation for life; education is life itself."

THE REMAINING CHAPTERS

This book has not been designed as the final word on the field of adult and continuing education nor even as a comprehensive statement on the profession, its aims, and its programs. Rather, the information is intended as an introduction to education and the adult learner. It presents the field of adult and continuing education as a leading force in both the historical and current movement toward a lifelong learning society. The book should be only one resource which the self-directed and, hopefully, interested learner will utilize. To that end, each chapter in this book will contain any necessary definitions, several study questions, and suggestions of additional resources. A brief description of the remaining chapters follows.

The second chapter presents a discussion of the societal role prescribed for, and assumed by, the adult and continuing education profession. Included is a discussion of the historical importance of adult and continuing education and how this history has shaped continuing education in the United States today.

The chapter also contains an analysis of the changing American society, the character of the American citizen, and the role of continuing education in helping the modern family. The chapter concludes with an analysis of why adult education is needed, a description of various obstacles to adult education, and a discussion of several implications for teacher education.

Chapter 3 will describe the clientele being served in adult and continuing education programs and activities. It will include a discussion of some unique qualities of the adult learner and a description of several categories of adult learners. The chapter also contains a discussion of the many undereducated or disadvantaged adults and of limited educational opportunities for the elderly person. The chapter concludes with some suggested implications for teachers.

The fourth chapter will present a picture of the various adult and continuing education programs available in the United States. Federal, state, and community-level programs will be described.

Chapter 5 contains a description of the professional educators who work with the various continuing education programs. Included is a discussion relative to who is an adult and continuing educator, what are the various types of available positions or roles, and how are these individuals trained for their work.

Chapter 6 presents information pertaining to the relationship between the American community and adult education. It will describe the problems of people at the community level, the availability of resources for education in communities, and how these educational resources can be activated in the pursuit of lifelong learning. A variety of implications for education are also described.

The seventh chapter presents an introduction to the theoretical bases and research important to adult education.

The final chapter describes various trends and projections related to society, higher education, and adult education. It also contains a discussion of various adult education needs and suggests several opportunities for educators.

SOME DEFINITIONS

Adult—A person who has reached the maturity level where he or she has assumed responsibility for himself or herself and sometimes others and who typically is earning an income.

Adult education—The relationship between an adult student and an educational specialist trained to work with adult learners in which the specialist provides the student with specialized information, learning experiences, or reference to resource materials. Frequently, such activities take place in the evening hours.

Continuing education—Often referred to in connection with or synonymous with adult education, the term has come to mean for many the extension of higher education programs to adult students. In this book, adult education, continuing education, and adult and continuing education will have synonymous meanings.

Education—The provision of instructional situations where the intent is that information, knowledge, and learning skills are acquired.

Educative community—The utilization and availability of a variety of community resources for learning and education.

Learning—The acquisition of knowledge, attitudes, and skills, usually resulting in behavioral change in an individual.

Learning society—The provision of purposeful learning opportunities both within and outside of the traditional educational institutions. In such a setting, formal education could be obtained throughout one's life.

Lifelong learning—A process of learning that continues throughout one's lifetime, depending on individual needs, interests, and learning skills.

Schooling—The provision of educational opportunity in a formal setting for some predetermined length of time.

STUDY STIMULATORS

1. What are the skills involved in lifelong learning? Are they intellectual skills, personal skills, or adaptive skills?
2. Should there be a qualitative dimension to such skills?
3. How could such skills be acquired by an individual? How should they be acquired?
4. What concepts of learning and what portion of the theory base from the current K–12 field of education should be incorporated into an evolving body of knowledge related to lifelong learning?
5. What kinds of changes will adult and continuing educators need to make in a lifelong learning society? What kind of changes will learners need to make?
6. What are some basic interdisciplinary concepts that can be applied in a variety of learning settings?
7. What is the relationship of the home environment and the family to lifelong learning?
8. Will there need to be societal changes before lifelong learning becomes a reality? If so, what kinds of changes?

SELECTED BIBLIOGRAPHY

Carnegie Commission on Higher Education. *Toward a Learning Society*, New York: McGraw-Hill, 1973. 112 pages. Appendix. References. This book describes the tremendous activity of a post-secondary nature. Lifelong learning, adult education, and alternative modes of education are also discussed. The book concludes by describing some objectives and priorities.

GOULD, SAMUEL B., and CROSS, K. PATRICIA (eds.). *Exploration in Non-Traditional Study*. San Francisco: Jossey-Bass, 1972. 137 pages. Index. This book contains a series of background essays prepared for the Commission on Non-Traditional Study. Problems of access, recognition, and the external degree programs are discussed. Another related book is the commission's *Diversity by Design*, 1973.

HESBURGH, THEODORE, M.; MILLER, PAUL A.; and WHARTON, CLIFTON R., JR. *Patterns for Lifelong Learning.* San Francisco: Jossey-Bass, 1973. 135 pages. Index. Bibliography. Appendix. This book is the work of a task force that studied continuing education and the future. It is divided into three sections. Section 1 looks at the future by describing a learning society and needed policy changes. Section 2 describes the role of higher education in the learning society. The final section describes some organizational and institutional needs to establish a lifelong learning system.

HOULE, CYRIL O. *The External Degree.* San Francisco: Jossey-Bass, 1973. 214 pages. Index. Bibliography. The author describes the emergence of the external degree in the United States. He also talks about some related issues, policy needs, and general problems. The bibliography is written in essay form and contains much useful information.

ILLICH, IVAN. *Deschooling Society.* New York: Harper & Row, 1970. 116 pages. The author presents a thesis that the school must be disestablished because of his theory that obligatory school polarizes people without preparing them for a future of learning needs. Alternative learning modes are described.

LONG, HUEY B., et al. "Lifelong Learning," *Journal of Research and Development in Education*, 7, No. 4 (Summer 1974). 110 pages. The entire theme of this issue is lifelong learning, with ten different authors contributing articles. Higher education, government, community adult education, aging, and technology are some of the topics covered in relationship to the lifelong learning movement.

OHLINGER, JOHN, and McCARTHY, COLLEEN. *Lifelong Learning or Lifelong Schooling?* Occasional Papers—No. 24. Syracuse, N.Y.: Publications on Continuing Education, Syracuse University, 1971. The authors present a view of the ideas of Ivan Illich and include an extensive annotated bibliography.

ROGERS, CARL R. *Freedom to Learn.* Columbus, Ohio: Charles E. Merrill, 1969. 358 pages. Index. Bibliography. Rogers's thesis is that education must facilitate more freedom in and out of the classroom. He talks about interpersonal relationships, values, and the teaching and learning process. A plan for self-directed change and self-directed education is included.

TOFFLER, ALVIN. *Future Shock.* New York: Random House, 1970. 505 pages. Index. Bibliography. This book is about what is presently happening to many people who are overwhelmed by change. The author explores how this change affects the communities in which we live, the organizations to which we belong, and our associations with one another. Some suggestions for coping with the rapidity of change are offered.

CHAPTER 2

The Societal Role of Adult and
Continuing Education

THE HISTORICAL IMPORTANCE OF ADULT EDUCATION

Historians have long known and written about the educational pursuits of the adult person. Education of the preliterate person in history was associated with religion. The notable societies that developed in Greece, Rome, Europe, and Great Britain facilitated study, expression in the arts, and personal growth for the elite or privileged person throughout his or her life. Thus, it can be argued that adult education has always been a natural part of civilization.

The American Story

Adult and continuing education has been an important part of many people's lives since the beginning of the American society. From what is known of life in the United States during the 1600s and 1700s, lifelong learning was a necessity because of the continued need for skilled people and because of the struggle for maturity as an independent country.

One of the earliest known adult education institutions was the Junto, a discussion club started by Benjamin Franklin and a few of his friends. The purpose of the discussions was to explore a variety of intellectual problems in the pursuit of self-growth and improvement. The first American public library is thought to have been an offshoot of the Junto organization.

The lyceum movement in the early 1800s was another important contributing force to the development of adult education in the United States. Initiated by a Mr. Josiah Holbrook in Connecticut, lyceums were local study groups with the purpose of facilitating self-improvement of participants. Speakers' bureaus, local service clubs, parent-teacher associations, and the Great Books study groups were influenced in some way or descended from the lyceum movement.

The Chautauqua movement developed in the late 1800s was an adult education pioneer effort that eventually affected small towns and rural areas throughout the United States. Originally conceived of as a religious adult education summer school for Sunday school teachers on Lake Chautauqua in western New York State, the concept became so popular that the intent and programs were enlarged to provide education on a variety of topics. Eventually, the notion of providing lecturers, cultural experiences, and entertainment was made mobile and brought to small towns and rural areas throughout many parts of the country by means of a tent show circuit. Although most of the Chautauqua movement ended by the turn of the century, the original Chautauqua Institutions still thrives and the tent show idea has been recently revived in some parts of the country.

There have been many other adult education programs or agencies of importance to the present-day state of the art that were initiated in the past century. The development of the Cooperative Extension Service, university extension programs, public libraries, and Americanization programs are only a partial listing of the many important branches of a developing field. The interested reader is referred to various bibliographic citations at the end of this chapter related to the history and development of adult education.

The 1950s and 1960s

The 1950s and 1960s are singled out as a special period because so many changes related to adult education occurred. Foundations began to take notice of the needs of adults throughout the country and gave support for a variety of adult and continuing education activities. The Carnegie Corporation, the Kellogg Foundation, and the Mott Foundation were some of the leaders in promoting adult education at the state and local community level. In addition, the Ford Foundation established and supported the Fund for Adult Education, an organization that promoted research, program and materials development, and a variety of experimental programs.

The Adult Education Association of the USA was formed in 1950. The National Association of Public School Adult Educators (now called the National Association for Public Continuing and Adult Education) was established in 1952. Together those two organizations have been primary forces in shaping the field as it is today. They supported research, developed or supported much of the recent literature of the field, provided a base for study and discussion pursuant to the growth of the field, and established a liaison relationship with federal and state programs.

Perhaps one of the most significant events to take place was the federal enactment of the Adult Education Act of 1965. The legislation provided federal support to, and recognition of, adult education as a necessary part of living. Adult Basic Education programs have been established in every state as a result, with nearly five million adults having been assisted through basic education by 1975. Approximately one million people each year are now being helped with the development of learning skills and increased abilities through ABE.

The act also has stimulated a variety of other programs, interest in adult education, and support at the state and local levels. General Educational Development (GED) programs for high school equivalency study, adult career education, adult basic education in a variety of institutions, increased educational opportunity for minority people and migrant workers, and increased general adult education activity in many agencies and organizations are a partial listing of the greater activity. Although many adults in the United States still possess inadequate educations and inefficient learning skills, the act gave a big boost to adult education.

The fifties and the sixties also were a period in which graduate adult education received much attention and experienced considerable growth. Chapter 5 explains in some detail the status of graduate programs for adult education throughout the United States. It should be noted here that professionalism in adult education, the development of a body of literature, and research specific to adult education obtained much impetus during the fifties and sixties.

How This History Has Shaped the Field

Almost every important development related to the adult education field has stemmed from an earlier development or has led to another major development. For example, vestigial elements of the Junto can be seen in the library. The lyceum, and even the Junto, had some influence on the Great Books study program. Literacy training for the enormous influx of immigrants during the early 1900s was eventually developed into the current Adult Basic Education program. Such linking aspects of the movement have provided shape and form to the field.

It is interesting to note, too, that the primary reasons for establishing adult education programs during the birth and beginning maturation of the country were the need for lifelong learning and the need for self-growth and self-expression. Both needs can be seen as the basic foundation for most adult education programs today (see Chapters 1 and 4).

Most of the important developments of an adult education nature that have taken place throughout this country's maturation have also helped to formulate a philosophy by which many adult educators operate today. This philosophy centers on the idea that each adult is a unique individual possessing unlimited potential. Thus, the role of the adult educator becomes one of helping individuals discover their own needs and of providing a learning environment where learners can meet their needs through such techniques as Great Books discussion, study groups, and the use of libraries and other community resources.

The early forms of adult education in the United States provided a solid foundation for the growth and maturation being experienced in present society. However, society continues to change and the adult education movement must change with it if the heritage of the present will be the historical foundation of a better tomorrow. The next section of this chapter and the final chapter contain additional discussion related to change and the future of adult education.

THE CHANGING AMERICAN SOCIETY

The dynamic quality of societal change is a reality faced by most people every day of their lives. The "Future Shock" theme, the problems of the cities, increasing bureaucracy and institutional complexity, rising crime rates and social disorder, and the frustrations of inflation coupled with energy crises are all grim reminders of the rapidity and complexity of social change. The purposes of this section will be to explore several aspects of the changing American society as they create forces related to current and future adult education needs.

Rural to Urban Movement

It should be no secret to any American that society has changed in its makeup drastically in the past few decades. A nation that was nearly 90 percent rural in the early 1900s is now almost entirely urban in makeup, with most of those remaining in rural settings very cosmopolitan in nature because of transportation, education, and communication advances.

The urban movement has remained dynamic, however, as many of those

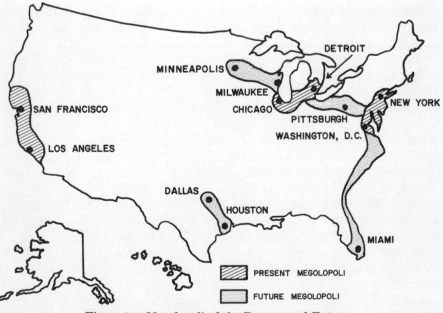

Figure 2.1. Megolopoli of the Present and Future

who become affluent move away from inner city areas toward the"suburbs." This has created sprawling residential complexes with concomitant problems related to public transportation needs, run-down inner city areas, and difficulties in maintaining a variety of city services.

The sprawling nature of urban growth has also resulted in systems of cities becoming tied together over huge masses of land. Referred to by some as megalopoli, these systems of cities have often resulted in unique city entities becoming almost indistinguishable from each other. Such settings already exist around larger cities, such as Dallas, New York, Chicago, Detroit, and Los Angeles. Experts suggest many more such settings are developing or will develop in the next two or three decades (see Figure 2.1).

The Character of Urban Communities

Nearly 70 percent of all the people in the United States live on about 1 percent of the land. Furthermore, such individuals are by and large very mobile in nature. Such a situation has resulted in what might be called a "tense" society. A tenseness that frequently erupts into violence, clashes of values, and peoples in constant search of personal values and a place in society.

Another characteristic of the urban community is the tremendous and rapid increase in the number of groups and organizations. If he or she wants, a person can belong to any number of local groups, some of which can be very diverse in nature. At the same time, due to the mobility and the closeness each separate community has with the total society because of rapid transportation and television, each person can have multiple contacts and affiliations with groups or organizations outside the local community. However, this situation of many group ties and links with outside forces often works to weaken individual ties to a locality and makes understanding the nature of the urban community quite difficult.

What will become of the nature of the urban community in future years? There is considerable evidence that urban communities will continue to change. Planned or experimental communities are being developed across the country. Such communities strive to provide most daily needs, including recreational opportunities, within short walking distance of one's home. Perhaps communities of this nature will become the norm in the future.

At the same time, there is increasing interest throughout the United States in revitalizing deteriorating urban cores of larger cities. A wiser use of land, multiple usage of such necessities as parking lots and city reservoirs, self-contained (most daily service needs contained within a complex) public and private housing complexes, and redoing worn-out or run-down inner city businesses are taking place in numerous locations. The careful planning and coordination of similar activities throughout the country should make the urban areas better places in which to live.

Changing Population Trends

Several demographic changes are taking place in the American society. The rapid and apparently unmanageable growth rates of only a few years ago have been reversed to the point that the United States has nearly achieved zero population growth. Such a phenomenon is advantageous for a number of ecological reasons, but the ramifications for our economy and for our educational system are not yet fully understood.

At the same time, people are definitely living longer. Longer lives usually mean longer periods of leisure. Consequently, several writers have wondered what will happen to our values and our place in the world if we become a leisure society. (Chapter 8 has more discussion of the amount of available leisure.) A related point is that senior citizens are increasingly demanding more rights, including the right for more adult education opportunities. The subsequent implications for the adult education profession are just beginning to be felt and are not very well understood thus far.

Another change taking place within the American population is the search for self-actualization. Call it the back-to-earth movement or a radical change in societal values, the fact of the matter is that an increasingly larger number of adults are studying new philosophies for life, are participating in self-awareness activities, and are experimenting with drastic changes in their lifestyles. (Chapter 8 also has more discussion on this change.) The challenge to adult and continuing educators is learning how to constructively facilitate efforts by adults related to personal growth and changing lifestyles.

THE CHARACTER OF THE AMERICAN CITIZEN

It should be obvious to the reader that the character of the American citizen cannot be adequately described in one small section of a single chapter. Throughout the United States there are Archie Bunker types, John Wayne heroes, liberated men and women, and average John or Jane Does. Such a mixture of individuals and the difficulties of a constantly changing American society make the provision of human services and educational programs a complex task.

The general well-being and steadily increasing Gross National Product (GNP) of the fifties and early sixties tended to give many people in the United States a fairly confident sense that all was well. It took the "Great Society" efforts of the mid-sixties to rock people out of their easy chairs. All at once, the total American society was made aware that masses of people lived in poverty, ghettoes, and despair, with little hope of ever changing their status. The paucity of efforts to help the "down and out" were subsequently replaced by a multitude of social action legislation and programs.

As one now takes a look nearly a decade later at this whole issue, several questions can be legitimately asked: What happened? Where did the tax dollar go? Why are there still so many disadvantaged, poor, and undereducated people in this country? The answers to these questions are not easy to find if, indeed, they can be found at all.

As a matter of fact, there is considerable evidence to support the contention that we have lost ground during the last ten years. A comparison of the 1960 census information with the 1970 census shows that very little progress was achieved in upgrading the educational level of the population. In addition, the poor are still poor and even more so—in fact, many people now suggest that we are closer than ever to a two-class society, the very rich and the very poor. Finally, the federal and state dollars available as support to the less-than-affluent are becoming more scarce every day because of revolts against high taxes, runaway inflation worries, and fears pertaining to the "welfare" society.

The character of the American citizen always seems to have been one of perserverance in the light of adversity, stubbornness in the light of immense obstacles, and confidence that any problem will eventually be solved. If such a character is to prevail it would appear that a considerable effort will be needed as this society completes its bicentennial and starts a third 100 years. It is the contention of this author that each person's relationship to lifelong learning will be an important ingredient in making such an effort successful.

THE MODERN FAMILY'S LIFELONG LEARNING NEEDS

The Changing Family Structure

The structure of the American family is in an apparently constant stage of evolution. The mobile nuclear family, the disappearance of the extended family, the ever-increasing divorce rate, the large number of married couples with only two, one, or even no children, and the variety of experimental family arrangements being tried throughout the United States are some of the current features of this change.

Within the nuclear family setting itself, considerable change also has taken place in the past one or two decades. Although observable differences in the roles played by fathers and those assumed by mothers still exist, many fathers are moving away from an "authority" stance to one of a loving, caring parent who acts toward the child in many ways similar to the mother. In addition, an increasingly larger number of mothers are working outside of the home. Many others have experienced a new concept of self and personal worth that has resulted in a different relationship with children and husband in the home.

Even given the change that has taken place and the change that will no doubt continue to occur, the demise of the family unit does not seem likely. At least 90 percent of all residents in the United States live in a family setting. In addition, the 1970 census revealed that there was even a 10 percent increase in the number of families compared with 1960 figures. The family structure will most likely survive as a basic institution of American life.

What the evolutionary change of the American family will produce in the future is only speculation at this point. What is clear, however, is that the changes of the past few years have put new demands on parents and their roles in contributing to the development of children in the home. Most of these demands and roles are related to the initial and continuing education of the children.

The Family's Role in Education

Each child's initial look at life is through the family setting. Basic needs of food, shelter, safety, and love are fulfilled primarily by parents in the home environment. In addition, in the early years of life a person is taught values, learns what is expected of self and others, and has individual abilities fostered.

Perhaps the most important function of parents is nurturing the intellectual development of their children. One researcher found that the following development takes place in terms of the amount of intelligence that can be measured by age 17: About 50 percent of such development takes place between conception and age 4.[1] In addition to playing a role in stimulating intellectual growth, parents are also important ingredients in the development of a child's physical, social, and emotional growth.

Thus, from a purely educational view the first few years of life are extremely important; later success in life is often related to the roles parents played in that early life and to the type of attitudes toward education and lifelong learning that were nurtured in the home. Education through the school setting is, of course, extremely important, but there must be a link between what transpires in the home in terms of intellectual development or attitudes toward learning and what exists in the classroom. Adult educators can play an important role in helping to link the family and the school.

The Role of Adult Education in Helping Parents

The above discussion points to some of the many reasons why educators and parents need to work together closely. The education and stimulation of youth is a tremendous task that requires cooperation by all adults in a community. It begins with knowledgeable parents creating a learning environment in the home, continues with school officials and parents cooperating on educational pursuits by children in and out of the home, and is supplemented by adult educators continually facilitating growth through parent education programs.

A variety of educational programs designed for parents already exist in many communities throughout the United States. Adult educators also need to establish educational opportunities within which parents can learn more

1. Benjamin Bloom, *Stability and Change in Human Characteristics* (New York: John Wiley, 1964), p. 88.

about the community and its many resources available to supplement the
intellectual and physical development of the child from birth to adulthood.
Such educational activities would be especially important when the child is of
preschool age because so much is learned and most attitudes about learning
are formed before a person ever enters the formal classroom.

A variety of learning opportunities are possible in almost any community:

Family tours in local industries to observe various career opportunities.
Visits to nature centers to study ecology.
Use of the Y programs or local parks for physical development.
Regular use of the library to stimulate reading.
Art gallery and museum visits to better understand culture and history.
Participation in musical activities to stimulate musical interests.

Numerous additional opportunities are possible. Many such opportunities
become continuing education for parents and can fill a variety of educational
needs not already being met through existing programs or institutions.

Learning to utilize the community as a supplemental setting for the education of children and for adults will require planning and coordination. The
various community activities suggested and the many others possible for
families will be effective in stimulating learning only if they are made effective
by knowledgeable parents and integrated with what is taking place when a
child enters a classroom. Thus, the adult and continuing educator must work
closely with both the parent and the K–12 educator. Learning how to make
better use of the community and its resources for education will be explored in
greater depth in Chapter 6.

WHY SOCIETY NEEDS ADULT AND CONTINUING EDUCATION

The chapter's discussion thus far has been intended as a presentation of
some historical underpinnings of adult and continuing education, coupled
with a brief description of various educational needs related to the American
citizen, family, and community. The changing nature of society that has been
described requires that nearly every citizen gain new skills, new understand-
ings, and new intellectual orientations throughout his life in order to live
satisfactorily. The remainder of this section will point out some of the primary
reasons adult education activities are necessary for a society.

The most obvious adult and continuing education function is the theme of
this book and the focus of Chapter 1—the facilitation of lifelong learning.
Based on the premise that formal education confined to the first two decades
or so of a person's life cannot possibly prepare one for the constancy and
rapidity of change, lifelong learning becomes an imperative if each person is to
cope with the explosion of knowledge, understand societal differences as they
evolve, and adapt to the aging process. Thus, adult educators must help

people keep their learning skills sharp and provide the best possible facilitative environment for learning.

Related to the above are subsequent changes in business and industry and the need for career training and retraining. Many people face several different careers in a lifetime because of changing interests or certain occupations becoming obsolete. In addition, many professionals such as those in medical and health areas must constantly study and learn if they are to remain proficient. Adult educators have a tremendous responsibility in facilitating occupational training and education for the professionals.

Another societal role is related to the surprisingly low level of educational achievement in the United States. Many low-income individuals cannot get out of their ruts because of inadequate amounts of education or training, each state has a large number of individuals with virtually no education at all, and, as indicated earlier, school dropout rates are increasing and in some states the average level of education has dropped in the past few years. Although increased education does not automatically mean a better life nor is education a panacea to cure all social ills, the adult educator has an important role to play in improving the literacy of many people.

Preparation for citizenship, or civic literacy as it is referred to by some, is another area of concern for the adult and continuing educator. Understanding one's own civil rights, becoming involved with community action or community development projects to solve a local problem, and simply being confident in communicating with others are important personal activities; thus, a variety of life skills are required if societal ills disliked by so many are to be cured.

A final need to be mentioned here relates to the increasing leisure experienced by some individuals that was mentioned earlier in this chapter. Hopefully, adult and continuing educators can increasingly find ways to help people fill their leisure with meaningful activities and learning pursuits designed for personal growth throughout a lifetime.

OBSTACLES TO ADULT AND CONTINUING EDUCATION

Although the societal role of adult and continuing education is immense, there are several obstacles that have prevented and are continuing to prevent lifelong learning from becoming a reality for all individuals. Four such obstacles will be described here. The reader is referred to various of the references cited at the end of the chapter for a more thorough discussion of the field, its potential, and its problems.

One critical problem is the relative secondary status or marginality of the field compared with K–12 education. A wide acceptance of adult education as a field of study or as a profession has been slow in coming, although this situation is changing due to the worldwide interest in lifelong learning, the critical need by many for new knowledge, and the actual increasing enrollments throughout the United States in adult education activities. This marginal status has created difficulties for adult education in achieving local, state, and federal financial support and, to a certain extent, in working with other educational professionals.

Related to the above problem is the fact that the educational system established in the United States is primarily oriented to youth. Many of the past beliefs and some of the present beliefs related to education center on the argument that a person filled with a certain amount of knowledge and any resulting skills by the magical age of 16, 18, or 22 will be prepared for life. Such a circumstance does not allow for new learning needs caused by changing occupational needs, the rapidity of change, and the changing adult personality described in other parts of this book. The point of this argument is that learning is indeed lifelong and that learning skills and positive attitudes toward continuous learning are extremely important goals for educational efforts aimed at a youth population.

Another problem facing adult educators in their efforts to serve the adult person is the fear of, or dislike for, school that preoccupies many people. Because of failures in early schooling, dissatisfaction with certain teachers or subjects, and the expectation that adult education simply will be an extension of earlier education, the adult educator often has difficulty in recruiting certain individuals into educational programs. Such a situation should change as the idea of lifelong learning becomes more widespread and as educators become more skilled at facilitating learning activities in other than the traditional classroom setting.

There are additional obstacles to adult education, as the interested reader or person working in the field will soon discover. For example, increased support must be found, new resources for education must be developed, and education must be made purposeful, convenient, and integrated with the normal pursuits of living. Overcoming the obstacles will be a difficult task. Hopefully, this book—when read by teachers in training, experienced K–12 educators, adult educators new to the field, and other interested individuals— will make a small contribution in further establishing adult and continuing education as a societal necessity.

IMPLICATIONS FOR TEACHER EDUCATION

Perhaps the most important implication of the discussion thus far is simply the need for teachers and administrators who work or will work primarily in K–12 programs to be aware of the tremendous need for, and growing involvement of, people in adult and continuing education. This would include helping K–12 students understand the need for lifelong learning and perhaps even encouraging parents to utilize adult education as a means for personal growth.

Related to developing an appreciation in students for continuous education throughout life is the development of a love for learning and numerous corresponding tools for learning. Such tools would include self-inquiry skills, the ability to undertake independent study, a curiosity about life, and knowledge regarding how to utilize a variety of resources for learning that exist outside of the normal classroom. Obviously, most schools of education throughout the United States are already helping teachers to foster the development of such tools in youth, but it is suggested much more can be done.

Another implication is related to parent education in follow-up to earlier discussion in this chapter. The impact of the parent and family environment in the early years, the ability of the parent to supplement at home education that takes place in the school, and the attitude about education and learning that parents transmit to their children are all factors with which the teacher must deal. Consequently, it is suggested that teachers work with parents even closer than they do now and that parents be encouraged to utilize adult and continuing education opportunities for their own personal growth and improvement as parents.

Finally, the increasing interest by many adults in self-growth as evidenced by enlarging enrollments in related educational programs suggests that a new educational lifestyle is indeed emerging—one in which learning is being looked to not only for vocational reasons but also for personal growth reasons. Educators at all levels have a crucial role to play in assisting with such an evolution and helping to bring about a society based on lifelong learning.

STUDY STIMULATORS

1. Determine the historical development of adult education in your local community.
2. Are there any Great Books discussion clubs administered through your local public library or elsewhere within the community?
3. Determine if any older persons residing in your community ever participated in the Chautauqua tent shows. Interview one or two persons regarding their experiences if you find some who did participate.
4. Are there ABE and/or GED programs in your community?
5. What is the level of educational attainment in your county or state? How many adults have less than an eighth grade education? Less than a fourth grade education? No schooling at all?
6. What has been the growth or change in population in your own community during the past two to three decades?
7. Describe as many as possible of the various types of experimental family arrangements being tried in the United States.
8. What types of parent education programs are available in your community? How would you change parent education opportunities in your community?
9. Design some possible family educational activities for your community. How

could they be integrated with, or made supplemental to, regular school activities?

10. Interview a local doctor, dentist, or some other professional working in a field of rapid change. Determine how they continue their own education.

SELECTED BIBLIOGRAPHY

GRATTAN, C. HARTLEY. *In Quest of Knowledge*. New York: Association Press, 1955. 337 pages. Index. This thorough book describes the history of adult education. Starting with the preliterate person, the author traces the development of education of adults through the Greek, Roman, and British societies. The final two-thirds of the book is devoted to the development of adult education in the United States.

HIEMSTRA, ROGER P. *The Educative Community: Linking the Community, School, and Family*. Lincoln, Nebr.: Professional Educators Publications, 1972. 116 pages. Appendixes. Annotated bibliography. This book is built around the premise that numerous resources for education exist in each community and that means for activating the educative community need to be found. Chapters describing the community, the community education movement, and the family's role in education are included.

KNOWLES, MALCOLM S. *The Adult Education Movement in the United States*. New York: Holt, Rinehart & Winston, 1962. 335 pages. Index. Bibliography. This book presents the history of adult education in the United States as a means of describing how the field has been developed. The nature and future of the adult education movement is also presented.

LeMASTERS, E. E. *Parents in Modern America*. Homewood, Ill.: Dorsey Press, 1970. 232 pages. Index. Written in realistic and lively terms, this book offers a critical review of the various literature on parent and child relationships. The author suggests that most books have tended to be child-centered and have not approached parenthood from the parent's point of view. Various chapters discuss such topics as folklore about parenthood, changes in parent roles, and parental models.

LIVERIGHT, A. A. *A Study of Adult Education in the United States*. Boston: Center for the Study of Liberal Education for Adults, 1968. 138 pages. This book provides an overview of the field of adult education and its many activities. An examination of various trends affecting adult education with suggested recommendations is included.

MICHAEL, DONALD N. *The Next Generation: The Prospects Ahead for the Youth of Today and Tomorrow*. New York: Random House, 1965. 207 pages. Index. Appendixes. This book examines various trends in the American society in an attempt to analyze where they are heading. Such topics as the economy, technology, marriage, education, and leisure are examined.

CHAPTER 3

Adult and Continuing Education:
Its Clientele

THE ADULT LEARNER DISCOVERED

Currently, the center of educational gravity appears to be shifting away from traditional schooling programs. For example, many public and private K–12 schools are facing declining or static student populations. In most parts of the country, colleges and universities are also experiencing decreasing enrollments in their regular undergraduate programs. Decreasing enrollments, fewer educational investment dollars, and demands for service from special groups such as the elderly and the poor have worked in concert to help educators suddenly "discover" the adult client.

That a great hunger for learning and educational opportunities exists in this country is reflected not only by the changes above, but also by the lifelong learning forces presented in the first chapter. In addition, there are many known statistics about need, interest, and involvement that support the hunger suggestion and serve as partial bases for the increasing enrollments and programs.

For example, the Commission on Non-traditional Study from the U.S. Office of Education has studied the involvement of adults in learning activities during the 1970s. The group discovered that a great upsurge of involvement is taking place. They now estimate that enrollments in public school adult education programs are growing at approximately 11 percent each year. They have also estimated that at least 15 million adults are enrolled in formal educational programs. These figures are in agreement with those furnished by the National Center for Educational Statistics (see Table 3.1).

The commission also estimated that when all the various learning endeavors outside of formal adult education programs are examined, at least 32 million persons undertook some form of adult study during the year 1972. The immensity of learning activity by adults comes into even sharper focus when added to these figures are the probable increases since 1972, the many adults involved in independent study,[1] and the special groups of people with need described in the first chapter.

1. Allen Tough (see Bibliography) has estimated that as high as 70 percent of all adult learning is of a self-directed nature. Consequently, because a large percentage of such learning would take place outside an institutionalized setting, the amounts shown in Table 1 most likely reflect only a portion of the actual learning activity undertaken by adults each year.

TABLE 3.1

TOTAL ADULT (17 AND OLDER) PARTICIPATION IN INSTRUCTIONAL SOURCES OF
ADULT EDUCATION, UNITED STATES, MAY 1969

Instructional Source	Number of Men	Number of Women	Total Number
Public or private school	1,557,000	2,081,000	3,638,000
College or university part-time	1,853,000	1,459,000	3,312,000
Job training	2,558,000	1,056,000	3,614,000
Correspondence courses	736,000	315,000	1,051,000
Community organizations	573,000	1,191,000	1,764,000
Tutor or private instructor	266,000	492,000	758,000
Miscellaneous activities	701,000	647,000	1,348,000
Totals	8,244,000	7,241,000	15,485,000

SOURCE: Imogene E. Okes, *Participation in Adult Education*, 1969, Initial Report (Washington, D.C.: U.S. Government Printing Office, U.S. Department of HEW, Office of Education, National Center for Educational Statistics, 1971).

Another indication of growing interest in the adult learner stems from a societal recognition of some crucial needs. As an example of this recognition, the National Advisory Council on Adult Education examined census information and other statistics to discover that in 1970 almost two million adults in the United States had never completed any formal schooling. The information also revealed that approximately 45 million adults over 25 years of age do not have a high school diploma. In addition, the poverty of millions, the coping dilemma of the aged, the institutionalized, or the handicapped, and the frequent job retraining or upgrading engaged in by many workers are constant reminders of learning need. A variety of federal, state, and local efforts are now underway in an attempt to upgrade some of these learning deficiencies.

THE UNIQUENESS OF THE ADULT LEARNER

To describe an adult learner in specific terms is impossible. There are almost as many different learning styles, needs, and rates of involvement as there are adults. It can certainly be said that every adult has the capability and potential for engaging in learning activities.

Current research is revealing that there are probably many more adults engaged in education and learning than has ever been tabulated by census bureaus and other agencies who identify educational enrollment numbers. A Canadian researcher, Allen Tough (see Bibliography) has investigated the participation of people in adult learning activities both in and out of institutionalized settings. By focusing on the individual and incidences of self-planned learning, he discovered that many adults spend 700–800 hours each year in recognizable learning endeavors. It is interesting to note, however, that Tough's research and the several follow-up studies by others have shown that a very large share of adult learning is both self-planned and separate from the typical adult classroom-related activity. Thus, many educators are beginning to pay attention not only to the uniqueness of the adult learner in terms of learning styles, but also to the tremendous interest in, and need for, self-directed, individual learning.

Why does this unique adult person need to be a continual learner? The answer to such a question is not an easy one to relay in only a few written sentences. Certainly, because each adult is a unique individual, he or she has some personal responsibilities to fulfill as a member of society, as a helper or provider to others, and as a man or as a woman. This encompasses the need for learning as liberal education, in developing oneself to cope as best as possible with the continual problems that plague humans, as a functional means of providing some meaning or bringing some joy to life, and in providing vocational/occupational skills.

One adult educator summarized this need to engage perpetually in learning activities by defining some goals for adult and continuing education:

To help the learner achieve a degree of happiness and meaning in life.
To help the learner understand himself, his talents and limitations, and his relationship with other persons.
To help adults recognize and understand the need for lifelong learning.
To provide conditions and opportunities to help the adult advance in the maturation process spiritually, culturally, physically, politically, and vocationally.
To provide, where needed, education for survival, in literacy, vocational skills, and health measures.[2]

The individuality of the adult learner also extends to the actual conduct of the learning activity. The growing body of knowledge and research central to adult and continuing education is replete with evidence of the adult's many unique characteristics, needs, and learning styles. (Chapter 7 discusses in greater detail some theory related to adult and continuing education.) The first and, perhaps, most important characteristic deals with the self-concept of the adult. For most, to be adult means to be independent, to possess a certain amount of self-motivation, and to be capable of making decisions about life and its problems.

A second important characteristic related to this uniqueness aspect is the wide and varied accumulation of experience with life that each adult possesses. A person engaging in a learning activity does not do so with this experience slate wiped clean. Consequently, the type and amount of educational need

2. Paul Bergevin, *A Philosophy for Adult Education* (New York: Seabury Press, 1967), pp. 30–31.

will vary, as will each person's desire or ability to bring this experience to bear upon the learning endeavor.

Each adult also will have a variety of problems or limitations that contribute to his or her uniqueness. Just the simple variable of age will impinge on each person differently in terms of visual or hearing acuteness, learning ability, and the energy level required for engaging in learning. In addition, the problems of life that one faces do not disappear when engaging in an educational endeavor and will undoubtedly affect such learning factors as retention, interest, and comprehension ability.

The fear of the new, the uncertainty of pushing back boundaries, and the remembrance of past learning failures or unsatisfactory experiences also will affect the adult engaged in learning. Becoming convinced that learning is a lifelong pursuit and a necessity will take place on very much an individual timetable.

Understanding the uniqueness of the adult learner is a necessary requirement for effectiveness with the teaching/learning process or in developing educational resources. More specific information on the teaching/learning process will be contained in later chapters; however, it seems necessary here to make the point that educators must reckon with the freedom and dignity of each person in society. This is based on the premise that each individual needs to be free to realize his or her own potential and that the success of a society is predicated on the interdependence of all its members. Consequently, a teaching and learning process for adults must be built to respond to the unique needs of those engaged in it.

CATEGORIES OF ADULT LEARNERS

There are different categories of adult learners, although no one category is mutually exclusive or all-encompassing. However, the purpose of suggesting some differences as to why people engage in learning is to highlight some implications for the entire teaching-learning process.

Houle completed a classic study of adults and why they engage in learning several years ago.[3] He determined that there were at least three distinct types of learners—distinct in the reasons ascertained for undertaking some educational endeavor. Within each category there will no doubt be differences based on such variables as age, sex, level of educational attainment, and other similar characteristics. However, the three categories provide a means for understanding something about the nature and actions of those people who actively engage in formal learning activities. A fourth category is added to reflect current research findings on learning outside of formal opportunities.

3. Cyril O. Houle, *The Inquiring Mind* (Madison, Wisc.: University of Wisconsin Press, 1963).

Goal-Oriented

A very visible type of learner is one who has some particular goal in mind as a basis for undertaking some learning activity or activities. Such a goal might be the desire to obtain a driver's license, a high school diploma, or a college degree. Very often such goals are related to one's occupation. The point is that the learner can justify or tie each learning endeavor to a distinct purpose felt necessary or important.

Activity-Oriented

The activity-oriented learner is one who engages in some educational endeavor because he or she just plain loves going or doing. Because of loneliness, because of a boring day, because of wanting to be with others, or various other similar reasons, certain people seem to thrive on social contact or involvement.

Learning-Oriented

This category is an interesting one to think about but its learners are more difficult to describe. Here is where can be found the truly continuing or lifelong learner. People in this category enjoy learning for its own sake, they typically read a lot, they make use of the community library, the museum, or other similar resources, and they often seem to have an interest in a never-ending number of subjects.

Self-Directed Learner

Not in one of Houle's originally conceived categories, the self-directed learner described earlier in the chapter is certainly becoming recognized by adult and continuing educators as a highly active participant in the total domain of adult learning. No doubt, this type of learner has always been around, but because programs, agencies, and enrollees are something visible or countable, the self-directed learner has not been fully recognized or easily recognizable. Suffice to say at this point, however, the self-reliant, autonomous, and independent learner now has the attention of adult education professionals.

Certainly there is considerable overlap in all four categories described above. It is highly probable that learners move through each category, depending upon their needs, their stage of development, or the availability of learning resources. In addition, it is just as probable that many more categories will emerge as the learner becomes better understood.

THE UNDEREDUCATED-DISADVANTAGED ADULT

The undereducated or disadvantaged adult presents a continual and plaguing problem within the American society—a problem that deserves special mention because of its pervasiveness and impact economically and socially. Many of the country's unemployed are in the jobless situation because of a lack of proper training. Most poor people and many minority people in the United States are unable to read well enough to compete adequately with the literate majority. Thus, in a society that can put men on the moon, that sees billions spent each year on entertainment, and that can produce consumer goods at a rate considerably higher than elsewhere in the world, the educational deficiencies are difficult to understand.

This dilemma is highlighted even more starkly by examining some known statistics. Nearly 24 million adults in the labor force (see Table 3.2) reported for the 1970 census that they had never completed high school. This is a staggering reminder of the misery existing below the glittering facade that is displayed as the American way of life.

TABLE 3.2

ADULTS (16 AND OLDER) IN THE UNITED STATES[a] LABOR FORCE[b] WITH LESS THAN A HIGH SCHOOL EDUCATION AND NOT CURRENTLY ENROLLED IN SCHOOL

Grade Level Completed	Male	Female	Total
0–5	292,700	153,600	446,300
6–8	7,751,500	3,303,200	11,054,700
9–11	7,817,300	4,645,000	12,462,300
Totals	15,861,500	8,101,800	23,963,300

[a] Labor force participants only.
[b] Does not include the states of Illinois, Indiana, and Wisconsin.

SOURCE: 1970 Census. Compiled by the National Institute of Education and referenced in *Annual Report* (Washington, D.C.: National Advisory Council on Adult Education, 1974).

Such a reminder is only partial recognition of the total situation. When all states are examined and the non-labor force persons are included, nearly one-fourth of the 203 million adults, 16 years of age and older in 1970, revealed that they had less than a high school diploma.

The lack of a formal diploma and/or a low level of educational accomplishment is not the only problem plaguing the disadvantaged adult. Problems of job obsolescence, unemployment or layoffs, and low-paying jobs are other difficulties faced daily by many people. Other related problems are as follows:

The number of school dropouts (or pushouts) is on the increase in the United States.
The numbers of individuals requiring some type of federal money support are growing.
Many elderly poor are without marketable skills that could be utilized in supplementing fixed incomes.

Many minority individuals find themselves forced into academic settings of a quality poorer than those established for the majority; the legislative correction measures will take years before equality is actually achieved.

The breadth of problems facing the undereducated or disadvantaged adult has only been partially sketched out here. However, the point is that a large task remains if the educational resources of this country are to be harnessed for more viable utilization in solving some of these problems. The opportunities for the educational field, and for adult and continuing education more specifically, are immense. Hopefully, such opportunities will not be overlooked.

THE OLDER ADULT

The largest minority group in the United States is the elderly and it is growing larger each year. Yet equal educational opportunity for the older person is more a myth than a reality. As Table 3.3 shows, in 1969 only 4.5 percent of the people age 55–64 and only 1.6 percent of those over 64 participated in formal adult education programs. Such percentages may have increased in the last few years and there are understandably many older persons engaged in self-directed learning, but the paucity of opportunity for the older person and low participation rates in educational programs deserve special attention in this chapter.

There are several problems the older person faces as a potential participant of adult and continued education. For example, transportation limitations and lack of mobility are often factors preventing participation in formal programs of education. In addition, of the total elderly population (over 64) living outside of institutions, 86 percent have some chronic health condition. While

TABLE 3.3

PARTICIPANTS IN FORMAL ADULT EDUCATION PROGRAMS AS A PERCENTAGE OF THE TOTAL ELIGIBLE POPULATION BY AGE, UNITED STATES, MAY 1969

Age	Population in Each Age Group	% Who Participated in Adult Education
17–24	24,800,000	18.0
25–34	23,600,000	18.2
35–44	22,700,000	13.5
45–54	22,700,000	9.4
55–64	17,900,000	4.5
65 and older	18,600,000	1.6

SOURCE: Imogene E. Oakes, *Participation in Adult Education*, 1969, Initial Report (Washington, D.C.: U.S. Government Printing Office, U.S. Department of HEW, National Center for Educational Statistics, 1971), p. 11.

the majority of the chronic conditions do not interfere to a great extent with mobility, 6 percent of the older population need to be assisted by another person and another 5 percent are housebound.

Many of the elderly are subjected to inadequate housing, poor nutrition, and substandard health care due to a low and usually fixed income level. As of 1972, there were more than two million individuals over the age of 65 who were considered functionally illiterate. More than 12 percent of the total elderly population had completed less than five years of school and of the racial minorities in this group, the percentage rose to nearly 40 percent.

The older person also faces various cognitive inhibitors to learning. Although there are many individual differences, some elderly people face declining memory potential, a slowing of conditional responses, and difficulties in sorting out learning that is based on long, sequentially related tasks. Some potential psychological limitations are lack of interest, fear of learning, and negative self-concepts.

Even given the variety of problems and low educational participation rates, there is available considerable evidence that the older person has a tremendous, mostly untapped, potential for learning. Community colleges and other institutions of higher education are beginning to offer special programs for senior citizens with considerable success in terms of the numbers enrolling. In addition, older persons are beginning to enroll in regular undergraduate programs throughout the United States.

A national study aimed at uncovering the extent of learning opportunity in a variety of agencies and organizations was completed recently in the United States.[4] Some 3,500 different programs were reported from all parts of the educational field and from a variety of non-school organizations. However, more than one-half of the programs were less than one year old at the time of the survey. Such findings indicate a rapid growth in opportunity and a recognition that the older person is a receptive client for adult and continuing education.

That the older person is an active learner and becoming even more active as opportunities are made available can be shown when their involvement in learning outside of institutionally sponsored programs is examined. The author recently completed an examination of more than 200 older people living in Nebraska. It was found that the average person over 55 years of age spends nearly 325 hours each year in some form of learning activity. However, more than 50 percent of that activity was informal, self-planned, and self-directed.

The older person has a need, yearning, and potential for active participation in lifelong learning. Strides are being made to help the elderly become full partners in educational activity. Hopefully, the educational field will continue to make available to people of all ages increasing opportunities and resources for learning.

4. Roger DeCrow, *New Learning for Older Americans* (Washington, D.C.: Adult Education Association of the USA, n.d. [1974]).

IMPLICATIONS FOR TEACHERS

Most of the implications that could be mentioned here are also related to the lifelong learning and teaching ideas expressed in Chapter 1. Consequently, they will not be repeated in this chapter. Instead, it will be the intent here to suggest some implications more specific to the uniqueness of adult clientele.

First, there is a need for experienced teachers, those being trained, and younger people considering education as a career to realize that a huge market for good teachers still exists. Perhaps some areas of specialization are currently overloaded; however, the growing need for educators of adults (as described in Chapter 1) might provide for some a career area to be considered.

A second point related to the first is the requirement that experienced and potential teachers must become familiar with the uniqueness of the adult learner. In addition to the several implications related to the adult as a learner suggested in the first chapter, the concept of self, the wealth of experience, the variety of real problems, and the various reasons for learning that the adult brings to the educational setting must be reckoned with by the teacher. Consequently, even more so than with younger people, the teacher who works full time, or even part time, with adults must be facilitator, needs-diagnoser, resource locator, counselor, and colleague.

A third implication has to do with the self-directed learning potential in adult students. If, in fact, many adults would prefer to do the most of their learning through self-directed endeavors, teachers will need to rethink their educational role. It will require giving up some of the rein, doing a better job of helping learners match their needs and interests with a variety of resources, and finding satisfaction with the job in ways other than immediate feedback from a large class of students. Such a change will require that teachers remove their institutional blinders and begin to think of the classroom as an open-ended laboratory for learning that can extend beyond a school building to a home, a factory, or a community.

SOME DEFINITIONS

Adult learner—Any adult who engages in some type of activity, formal or informal, in the acquisition of knowledge or skill, in an examination of personal attitudes, or in the mastery of behavior.

Disadvantaged adult—Individuals who are usually classified by any of the following terms: "poverty sub-culture person," "hard-core poor," "low-income person," "culturally deprived individual," "functionally illiterate person," "educationally deficient person," or the "hard-core unemployed individual."

Older adult learner—In this book, an older adult learner is a person 55 years of age or older who engages in some form of learning.

Self-planned learning—A learning activity that is self-directed, self-initiated, and frequently carried out alone.

STUDY STIMULATORS

1. What are some of the reasons for the rapid growth in the amount of study by adults through both formal and informal routes?
2. What are the statistics for your state relative to educational levels of the adult population and the number of people with less than a high school education? Are such levels harming your state? If yes, in what ways?
3. Discuss the goals for adult and continuing education described on page 33. Derive some additional goals you think would be important.
4. What can be done in the United States to solve some of the educational problems related to the undereducated-disadvantaged adult?
5. Determine and discuss adult education job opportunities, pay rates, and career advancement opportunities in your community or state.
6. Discuss various ways an educator might provide assistance to the self-directed learner. Should such an assistance be provided?
7. What educational opportunities for older people are available in your community?
8. What more can be done or should be done in your community to meet the educational needs of the older person?

SELECTED BIBLIOGRAPHY

ANDERSON, DARRELL, and NIEMI, JOHN A. *Adult Education and the Disadvantaged Adult.* Syracuse, N.Y.: ERIC Clearinghouse on Adult Education, 1969. 96 pages. Bibliography. The concern of the authors was to examine the role of education in altering the personal and social characteristics of disadvantaged adults. The book points out the many problems faced by disadvantaged people. The large bibliography is a useful tool for further study.

"Back to School for Millions of Adults," *U.S. News & World Report,* April 2, 1973, pp. 73–74. This article reports on the rapid growth of enrollments in various adult education programs throughout the United States.

HOULE, CYRIL O. *The Inquiring Mind.* Madison, Wisc.: University of Wisconsin Press, 1961. 87 pages. The author draws some landmark conclusions in this book based on intensive interviews with several adults. He has determined that there are three basic groups of learners: goal-, activity-, and learning-oriented individuals. Educators should find this little volume very useful in better understanding the clientele they must serve.

KNOWLES, MALCOLM A. *Self-Directed Learning.* New York: Association Press, 1975. 135 pages. Appendix. A description of self-directed learning and the competencies required for self-directed learning. The author describes how to design a learning plan, describes how educators can facilitate such learning, and has a whole section entitled "Resources," where he describes various exercises to improve learning skills and various learning techniques.

"Lifelong Learning: The Back-to-School Boom," *Saturday Review,* Special Section, September 20, 1975, pp. 14–29. This special section has some interesting information on enrollments, programs, and clientele. Four authors contribute an article apiece on "Educating New Majority," "The Nordic Example," "From Mel Brooks to Medicine 75," and "Adult Ed—The Ultimate Goal."

OKES, IMOGENE E. *Participation in Adult Education 1969 Initial Report.* Bulletin 1971, No. HE 5.213: 12041. Washington, D.C.: U.S. Department of Health, Education, and Welfare, Office of Education, U.S. Government Printing Office, 1971. This report is based on sampling data from throughout the United States. Numerous tables display adult education participants according to various demographic characteristics.

Perspectives of Adult Education in the United States and a Projection for the Future. Report of the third International Conference on Adult Education, Sponsored by the United Nations Educational, Scientific, and Cultural Organization, Tokyo, Japan, July 25–August 7, 1972. Washington, D.C.: Health, Education, and Welfare, U.S. Office of Education. 65 pages. Appendix. The book contains a discussion of the scope of adult education now, including its participants, role, organizational structures, and services. It also suggests some innovations and future directioning for adult education and learning.

TOUGH, ALLEN. *The Adult's Learning Projects.* Research on Education series No. 1. Ontario: The Ontario Institute for Studies in Education, 1971. 191 pages. Appendixes. Bibliography. This book represents a breakthrough in research on adult learning. The author has discovered that considerably more learning takes place by the average adult in a year than has been previously reported. Most of the learning, however, is self-directed and outside of any classroom setting. Implications, suggestions for working with the self-directed learner, and future needs are presented.

CHAPTER 4

Adult and Continuing Education:
Its Programs

THE NATURE OF ADULT EDUCATION PROGRAMS

The term "program" can be found in adult education literature to have several different meanings. In addition, practitioners who plan, teach, and implement adult education activities frequently may have many different definitions in mind when they describe their programs. The purpose of this introductory section is to describe some of the different conceptions of what "program" means and to provide a definition as a basis for the remainder of the chapter.

One common means for describing adult education programs is to refer to their institutional base: the YMCA program, the community college program, or the public school adult education program. However, this concept of program does not readily discriminate between those activities that are for youth and those that are for adults. In addition, some institutions may utilize adult education only to achieve an organizational goal not necessarily related to adults or to education, such as the training program in a business; another institution may view adult education as its primary function and focus. Consequently, comparisons of adult education programs among various institutions are difficult.

Another way in which adult education is at times referred to as a program is by the methodological format utilized in presenting information. In other words, it is not uncommon to hear of a workshop, retreat, or educational television presentation referred to as an educational program for adults. However, comparisons between activities of a methodological nature and those of the broader institutional view are practically impossible to make.

There are other means for describing programs and the reader is referred to several of the sources cited at the end of this chapter. For purposes of this chapter, the following definition is presented: *the total set of procedures, instructional techniques, administrative arrangements, and purposes necessary for the bringing together of educational opportunity and an adult with a learning need.* Such learning is implied to be purposeful, undertaken voluntarily, and supplemental to the main responsibilities of life. The sponsorship of programs may be at the federal, state, or community level.

Even the above definition does not distinctly categorize every learning activity engaged in by an adult. For example, the many self-directed and self-planned learning pursuits undertaken by a person in his or her lifetime may not fit completely within the definitional boundaries. In addition, many programs will operate across all three levels of sponsorship, while others operate at the very microphase of any one level. However, the broad definition and the three levels of sponsorship provide a base for describing most of the adult education activities in the United States.

FEDERAL PROGRAMS

There are several adult and continuing education programs that have their genesis at the federal level. Frequently, this genesis is in the way of financial support, leadership in the way of coordination, providing cohesion to the field, and governmental liaison, and the development of resource materials. Programs that actually involve adults are usually at the state and, most often, at the local community level. Consequently, the reader may need to make conceptual linkages among the three levels of sponsorship for certain of the programs.

The major programs, their aims, and their audiences will be described in the following subsections. All of the subsections under the three headings are relatively brief and general in nature. The reader is referred to the Bibliography at the end of the chapter for sources containing more specific information.

Extension Service, USDA

The federal Extension Service (ES) with offices in Washington, D.C., is a division of the U.S. Department of Agriculture. ES serves as a source of information to, and coordination for, extension programs at the state and local community. The federal organization also serves as a link to the legislative/political side of Washington life. The ES provides program ideas, research data, and expert assistance to states on a need and program forecasting basis.

The federal Extension Service also makes available some direct services to states and communities. Support and leadership is provided to the National 4-H Center, which trains young adults and Extension workers; financial support and leadership is provided to the Expanded Food and Nutrition Education Program (EFNEP), an adult education endeavor at the local community level which employs paraprofessionals; planning assistance is also provided to states through the national Extension Management Information System–State Extension Management Information System (EMIS-SEMIS).

Office of Education

The U.S. Office of Education (USOE) has a variety of divisions and programs related to adult education. Located in the U.S. Department of Health, Education, and Welfare, the Office of Education has adult and continuing education elements in the Bureau of Occupational and Adult Education, Division of Adult Education, Right to Read Office, and the Bureau of Post Secondary Education. Leadership, resource materials, and financial support are provided for such educational programs as Adult Basic Education, General Educational Development, Right to Read, Community Education, and Adult Career Education. Special programs of research and leadership training are also funded out of USOE.

USOE also supports several Educational Resources Information Centers (ERIC) throughout the United States. The purposes of the ERIC facilities include acting as a clearinghouse for educational research and other information, producing bibliographies and other informational reports of interest to the educational field, and stimulating educators to think through their informational needs. An ERIC Clearinghouse on Adult Education existed at Syracuse University until 1974. Now the ERIC Clearinghouse on Career Education at Northern Illinois University focuses on adult education, career education, and vocational education.

Manpower Training

The U.S. Department of Labor has provided leadership and financial support for a variety of manpower development programs. Utilizing such enabling legislation as the Economic Opportunity Act and the Manpower Development and Training Act, the department has helped to develop employment and training programs throughout the country. These have included such efforts as the Concentrated Employment and Training Program, the Job Corps, skill and on-the-job training in a variety of occupations, the Neighborhood Youth Corps, Operation Mainstream, and the Work Incentive Program.

Miscellaneous Programs and Organizations

Numerous additional programs with some elements of adult and continuing education exist at the federal level. The Appendix at the end of this chapter contains a listing of the various bureaus, departments, and agencies with one or more federally supported adult education or training programs.

There are other federal government programs that have a connection in some way to the adult education field. For example, the National Institute for Education (NIE) supports developmental or experimental research and programs in such areas as non-traditional education. The National Center for Educational Statistics (supported by the Office of Education) has an adult and vocational education branch that carries out research and population surveys on such topics as adult participants in education and instructional sources of adult education.

Appointed from the President's Office are two advisory councils that deal directly with adult and continuing education. The National Advisory Council on Adult Education and the National Advisory Council on Extension and

Continuing Education provide reports to the professionals in the field, carry out research related to adult and continuing education, and make recommendations to the President and other officials at the national level.

There are several professional associations that are described in greater detail in Chapter 5 whose activities include the development of national publications, liaison with federal government offices and officials, and coordination of various adult education activities. These include the Adult Education Association of the USA (AEA), National Association for Public Continuing and Adult Education (NAPCAE), National University Extension Association (NUEA), Commission of Professors of Adult Education (CPAE), Coalition of Adult Education Organizations (CAEO), and the National Community Education Association (NCEA). (The *1974 Directory of Resources in Adult Education* cited at the end of the chapter describes 37 professional associations that have a connection to the adult education field.) Numerous national foundations also provide financial support and encouragement for continuing education endeavors.

STATE AND REGIONAL PROGRAMS

A variety of adult and continuing education programs receive sponsorship or direction from states, regional groupings, or multi-state consortia. Often affiliated with or receiving funding from federal sources, the state and regional programs can focus on problems and clientele unique to a particular area.

State Department of Education

State departments of education typically have had a long affiliation with adult and continuing education efforts. They have provided special consultants to local communities, carried out record-keeping activities, and provided financial support to adult education activities throughout the states for some time.

More recently, the Adult Education Act of 1966 and various following amendments have allowed states to match some state and local monies with federal monies in the establishment of Adult Basic Education, General Educational Development (high school completion), and other educational programs for adults. Most states have one or more full-time professionals working with adult and community education programs.

Regional USOE offices provide liaison services from the federal government to the state offices. Until 1975 there also existed regional staff development programs or consortia whose purposes were to assist state departments of education in the training of adult education personnel. Such functions are now being undertaken by the state departments as a result of the most recent amendment to the Adult Education Act.

Military

The various military organizations carry out numerous adult and continuing education activities. The activities range from credit programs for military personnel to noncredit programs for interested people. Most of the programs are administered out of a primary military headquarters or base and therefore serve military and other clientele on a regional basis.

Professional Organizations and Associations

Most states have one or more professional adult and continuing education–related associations. Such groups usually provide consultative assistance to local communities, carry out at least one statewide conference each year, and maintain some sort of newsletter or periodic publication for members. The state associations often serve as the only device available for adult educators scattered throughout a state to have periodic contact with one another and to obtain continuing professional education.

There is a current movement in some states to merge all the various adult, continuing, and community education–related associations into one large state organization. The state of Nebraska, for example, has an association entitled the Adult and Continuing Education Association of Nebraska. The association has an affiliation with both AEA and NAPCAE at the national level. The state of Iowa recently merged its various adult education organizations into one group called the Iowa Association for Lifelong Learning.

Regional associations for adult education also exist. Their purposes are to supplement the various state associations' activities and to provide additional continuing professional education. Although varying from region to region, their activities usually include annual conferences and regional publications.

Miscellaneous Programs

Numerous additional statewide or regional programs of adult and continuing education exist. Various foundations, voluntary organizations, religious organizations, educational television networks, and governmental agencies operate educational programs for adults in most states. Training programs, public information efforts, and public awareness programs are the usual activities that are offered.

COMMUNITY PROGRAMS

The heart of adult and continuing education activity is programing at the community level. As Table 4.1 shows, numerous types of organizations are involved with adult education and many people are involved with the programs. The table's figures account for only part of the many educational programs for adults at the community level and do not reflect the rapid growth since 1972. For example, Adult Basic Education enrollments have grown from one-half million adults in 1969 to approximately one million students in 1974. In addition, more than 300,000 adults received a high school equivalency diploma or certificate based on General Educational Development (GED) test scores in 1974. Most adult education programs are in a state of rapid growth. The following subsections will briefly describe a variety of programs and the clientele they serve.

Community School and Community Education

Not even included in Table 4.1 are the many programs and people involved with community education programs. Typically, where community school–community education programs exist, a large percentage of the adults in that community participate in some fashion each year in learning activities. The programs often include a variety of credit and noncredit programs ranging from vocational training to recreational activities.

TABLE 4.1

ADULT AND CONTINUING EDUCATION IN COMMUNITY ORGANIZATIONS: 1972 DATA

Type of Organization	Number With Adult Education Programs[a]	Number of People Involved	% of Total
Churches	50,480	3,614,000	32.9
Other religious groups[b]	3,310	474,000	4.3
Y's and Red Cross	3,360	3,050,000	27.8
Civic organizations[c]	3,730	1,175,000	10.7
Social service groups[d]	4,350	2,285,000	20.9
Cultural and other groups[e]	1,540	370,000	3.4
Totals	66,770	10,968,000	100.0

[a] Adult education programs included those aimed at skill, knowledge, and attitude building. They included organized instructional efforts, primarily on a part-time basis, and did not include credit classes, in-service training efforts, and recreational activities.
[b] Church headquarters, council of churches, Salvation Army, youth centers, related homes for the aged, etc.
[c] Neighborhood centers, senior citizen groups, civil liberties groups, and others concerned with community issues and betterment.
[d] Social welfare groups, American Cancer Society, vocational rehabilitation, alcohol groups, etc.
[e] Social and literary societies, civic theater groups, symphony organizations, etc.

SOURCE: Evelyn R. Kay, *Adult Education in Community Organizations, 1972* (Washington, D.C.: U.S. Government Printing Office, U.S. Department of Health, Education, and Welfare, Office of Education, National Center for Educational Statistics, 1974).

The community education movement in the United States can be traced to various locales and experimental efforts. However, the effort that has probably made the greatest contribution is the Mott community school program which started in Flint, Michigan, in the 1930s. The Mott Foundation and a variety of other sources have helped to establish community education programs in many parts of the United States. Recently approved national legislation and various enacted state legislative bills related to community education should continue to aid in the development of adult and community education at the community level.

Public School Adult Education

Public School adult education programs historically have involved millions of adults in learning pursuits. Many communities in the United States still administer adult education through local school boards. The resulting activities include such programs as Adult Basic Education, vocational and agriculture education, general education, and recreation-related education. This situation is going through considerable change, however, as several communities across the country now have their public school adult education programs administered through or in conjunction with community education or community college activities.

Community Colleges

The community and junior colleges in the United States offer a variety of community service programs to adults. College transfer programs, general education opportunities, vocational training, noncredit adult programs, and learning resource centers are among the opportunities available to local community and supporting area residents. Most community colleges make an effort to coordinate their educational programs with the adult education efforts of other agencies.

University Extension

Most institutions of higher education throughout the United States offer credit and noncredit learning opportunities through university extension or continuing study programs. Correspondence courses, media services, on-campus and off-campus conferences, off-campus courses, and travel courses are frequent modes of education utilized for extension programs.

Some colleges and universities have residential centers for continuing and extension education activities. With such centers more extensive adult education programing can be undertaken. Workshops and institutes of longer duration than a typical conference are possible. In addition, food and hotel services allow participants opportunities for more intensive involvement in the learning activities.

Cooperative Extension

Receiving support from the federal Extension Service and state Cooperative Extension Service offices, most counties have Cooperative Extension Service offices where professionals plan and administer a variety of educational programs. Four areas, including agriculture, home economics, youth development, and community and resource development, make up the programing emphases. Specific program topics for adults include home and family living, agriculture and marketing, home and commercial gardens, general horticulture, foods and nutrition, clothing construction, consumer buymanship, money management, community and resource development, general home economics, and public affairs education.

One of the strengths of Cooperative Extension at the local community and county levels is the development and use of volunteer leaders. Various in-service training devices are utilized for leader development, and the volunteer leaders in turn assist with the planning, implementation, and evaluation of many educational programs for adults living in a county.

Libraries, Museums, and Art Galleries

Most adults living in the United States have at least one library, museum, or art gallery in their own or nearby community. Exhibits, books, lectures, and special displays are some of the most widely utilized modes of education for interested adults. Many of these organizations will also have one or more meeting rooms available for special programing needs. In addition, many libraries and some art galleries or museums have displays, books, or programs that can be taken to individuals who live in remote areas or who cannot easily travel to the primary site.

Many libraries, museums, and art galleries throughout the United States employ adult education or community specialists. These individuals administer special programs, work with community groups, and provide liaison services with other educational programs in a community. Services for the blind, tutorial assistance, film and recording services, Great Books discussion groups, and reader guidance are some of the special programs carried out by libraries. Some museum and art galleries hold adult classes, administer field trips, and offer special lecture series.

Private and Proprietary Schools

There is a variety of private and proprietary schools throughout the United States whose purposes are to provide special training to adults. These organizations offer training in a number of vocational and occupational areas through regular courses, correspondence education, and individual-to-individual tutorial service. Private learning centers, secretarial schools, barber schools, and skilled trade preparation programs are examples of the training being offered.

Business and Industry

A tremendous amount of adult education takes place through on-the-job training, apprentice programs, leadership development, preretirement programs, and continuing professional education efforts by business, industry, and labor unions in the United States. Many business and industry related organizations employ one or more persons whose functions deal primarily with training and education. In-plant education, time-release to attend educational programs, conference and workshop opportunities at various sites throughout the United States, and tuition reimbursement programs for credit and non-credit college or high school courses are some of the means by which employees may further their education.

Religious Education

As was shown in Table 4.1, churches and other religious organizations reach a large number of adults each year through educational programs. Courses, seminars, and study groups concentrate on such topics as Bible study, religious doctrine and heritage, philosophy, human values and relations, self-growth and awareness, and literature. Many larger churches and religious organizations employ one or more persons who are responsible for adult education activities and programs.

Programs for the Older Person

Many communities in the United States have special educational programs for older persons. Senior citizen centers, nursing homes, and various volunteer organizations or professional associations administer travel and tour programs, art and crafts activities, academic credit and noncredit courses, and recreational activities for interested participants. As has been noted in several of the preceding descriptions, the larger organizations often have the resources to employ one or more professionally trained educators to work with such programs.

Miscellaneous Agencies

In any given community, there might be one or more of the following agencies or groups sponsoring some sort of educational programs for adults:

Learning resource centers   Community action agencies
Voluntary associations   Welfare and public assistance agencies
Health organizations   Civic organizations
Community development agencies

In addition, private groups, individuals, and neighborhood associations often provide adult education programs, typically, however, in larger communities.

SOME PROBLEMS

There are many problems yet to be solved before the various adult and continuing education programs can be fully utilized in a lifelong learning sense. Solutions to these problems will not be easy to find or easy to implement.

One major problem is the lack of coordination of programing. Such a lack leads to a competition for clientele, often at the expense of meeting the educational needs of the adult audience. The problem exists most noticeably at the local community level, but often, too, at the state and national levels.

Another problem is the relatively low financial support for adult and continuing education in comparison to support for youth education and other forms of human service. Most taxpayers, for example, must support the free education of youth and, at the same time, pay for any adult education activities in which they engage. Financial support problems exist at the national, state, and local levels.

Determining how much lifelong learning opportunity to make available in each community is another area of concern. As a matter of fact, it is not uncommon to find programs planned and offered that are based purely on hunch or on what was tried in some other community. A related problem is keeping adult education programs from becoming so over-institutionalized to the point that they are always tied directly to a long-range curriculum plan, credentialism need, or methodological constraint. Such institutional limitations prevent the facilitation of educational needs possessed by self-directed learners.

A final problem to be discussed here in relation to adult education programs concerns the difficulties agencies and organizations have in maintaining top quality educational opportunities. Finding qualified teachers, determining the real needs of participants, and utilizing instructional approaches or techniques that are appropriate for the adult person are some of the issues related to quality programing that must be addressed. Later chapters will discuss such issues in greater detail.

SOME DEFINITIONS

Adult Basic Education (ABE)—Instruction in communicative, computational, and social skills for adults whose inability to utilize such skills lessens their obtaining or retaining employment commensurate with their real ability. In addition, a person's satisfaction with life may be greatly reduced by the lack of such skills. Formal ABE programs usually include instructions for adults whose educational attainment is below the eighth-grade level.

Adult education agency—An institution, organization, or group whose primary purpose is the facilitation of educational programs for adult clientele. Such an agency or group is often part of a larger institution.

Clientele—The specific subgroup of people for which an adult education agency aims its programs.

Course—A planned sequence of educational activities designed to give the participant new skills or knowledge. A course may be for credit or noncredit.

High school equivalency diploma—The General Educational Development (GED) tests service of the American Council on Education provides a high school equivalency diploma or certificate to individuals who pass the equivalency examination. High schools and state departments of education issue the diploma or certificate.

STUDY STIMULATORS

1. How many different meanings to the term "program" can you identify in your community or in reviewing some adult education literature?
2. List the different institutions offering adult education opportunities in your community. Analyze the different types of clientele served by each institution.
3. Determine the reasons for the development of the Cooperative Extension Service in the United States. What legislative basis does the Cooperative Extension Service have?
4. What is the current level of federal support for Adult Basic Education in your state? What is the level of state support? What relationship does your state department of education have with your local community's adult education efforts?
5. Analyze the different kinds of instructional methods used by institutions or agencies in your community that offer programs for adults.
6. Does your community have a community education or public school adult education program? If so, determine the extent and type of adult education opportunities.
7. What type of adult education opportunities are available through the community college in or nearest to your local community?
8. What kinds of educational opportunities for adults are available through your county Cooperative Extension Service office? (Visit the office if you have an opportunity.)
9. Visit a library, museum, or art gallery in your community or in a nearby community. What kind of adult education programs does the organization have?
10. Make a tally of the number of different proprietary or private schools in your community offering educational opportunities to adults.
11. Interview one or more church educators in your community. Determine the breadth and nature of educational opportunities for adults.
12. What type of adult education programs are available in your community for older persons? Are there any preretirement educational programs available in local businesses or through some other organizations?

SELECTED BIBLIOGRAPHY

Books
AXFORD, ROGER W. *Adult Education: The Open Door*. Scranton, Pa.: International Textbook Company, 1969. 247 pages. Index. Appendixes. The author provides an introduction to adult education, its leaders, its programs, and its place in society. Supportive materials, tables, and resource guides are included.

GRABOWSKI, STANLEY M., and GLENN, ANN C. *1974 Directory of Resources in Adult Education*. DeKalb, Ill.: ERIC Clearinghouse in Career Education, Northern Illinois University, 1974. 128 pages. The book contains a wealth of information pertaining to adult education associations, adult education periodicals, and graduate programs of adult education. In addition, the book contains some information on a variety of resources and the location of resources related to adult education.

JENSEN, GALE; LIVERIGHT, A. A.; and HALLENBECK, WILBUR (eds.). *Adult Education: Outlines of an Emerging Field of University Study*. Washington, D.C.: Adult Education Association of the USA, 1964. 334 pages. Appendix. The book has chapters on a variety of topics written by many authors. In addition to providing a general overview of the field of adult education, the book has some specific information on programs and institutions.

KNOWLES, MALCOLM S. (ed.). *Handbook of Adult Education in the United States*. Washington, D.C.: Adult Education Association of the USA, 1960. 624 pages. Index. This book has a variety of general information on the field of adult education. Each chapter was written by a different author. Two sections of the book are devoted to institutional programs, program areas, and resources in adult education.

————. *The Modern Practice of Adult Education*. New York: Association Press, 1970. 384 pages. Appendixes. Index. This book describes a unique teaching and learning process for use in working with adults participating in educational programs. Examples utilized throughout the book provide a wealth of information on various programs and the author includes a useful bibliography at the end of each chapter.

Marquis Academic Media. *Yearbook of Adult and Continuing Education, 1975–76*. Chicago: Marquis Academic Media, 1975. 566 pages. Subject and geographic indexes. The rapid growth of the field of adult and continuing education is reflected by this first edition of a yearbook. Much information is contained within the 566 pages, including various statistics and tables on the involvement of adults in educational programs, specific information on Adult Basic Education, reports of activity in continuing education and community service, and specific information on governmental support of, and involvement with, adult education.

SHAW, NATHAN C. (ed.). *Administration of Continuing Education*. Washington, D.C.: National Association for Public School Adult Education, 1969. 438 pages. Index. Appendixes. Written primarily for the administrator of public school adult education or community education programs, the book contains supporting information relative to different programs of adult education. A useful bibliography is included in the appendix.

SMITH, ROBERT M.; AKER, GEORGE F.; and KIDD, J. R. (eds.). *Handbook of Adult Education*. New York: Macmillan, 1970. 594 pages. Index. Appendixes. This book contains one of the most up-to-date discussions of the entire field of adult and continuing education. (A more current handbook series is now in production.) Institutions, organizations, and specific program areas related to adult education are described in numerous chapters, each written by a knowledgeable author. Specific programs such as community college, the Cooperative Extension Service, public libraries, business and industry, and many others are described. Essential for a professional adult education library.

An additional reference can be found in Chapter 2: Liveright.

Periodicals

Adult Education. Published quarterly by the Adult Education Association of the USA, Washington, D.C. The journal presents research information on all aspects of adult education.

Adult Leadership. Published monthly except July and August by the Adult Education Association of the USA, Washington, D.C. The periodical presents articles on a wide range of topics of interest to the adult education practitioner.

Other periodicals with more specialized audiences include the following:

Adult and Continuing Education Today   *Extension Service Review*
Community and Junior College Journal   *Journal of Extension*
Convergence   *The NUEA Spectator*
ERIC—Resources in Education   *Training and Development Journal*

APPENDIX

Federal Activities in Adult Education

Department of Defense—Available are various pre– and post–high school programs ranging from Adult Basic Education to college-level training.

Gallaudet College—Adult and continuing education programs for the deaf.

Department of Health, Education, and Welfare—The department has a variety of vocational, social and rehabilitational, and special-audience programs of adult education.

Department of Housing and Urban Development—Such programs as the Model Cities Manpower Programs and the Community Development Training Program have adult and continuing education elements.

Department of Interior—The Bureau of Indian Affairs has numerous educational programs for adults.

Department of Justice—The Bureau of Prisons sponsors some adult education activities.

Additional agencies administering programs with extension, continuing education, and community service features include the following: National Science Foundation, Department of Agriculture, Environmental Protection Agency, Atomic Energy Commission, Office of Economic Opportunity, Veterans' Administration, National Foundation on the Arts and the Humanities, Department of Commerce, Department of Labor, Tennessee Valley Authority, and Department of Transportation.

SOURCES: National Advisory Council on Adult Education, *Federal Activities in Support of Adult Education* (Washington, D.C.: National Advisory Council on Adult Education, 1972; and *Yearbook of Adult and Continuing Education*, 1975–76 [Chicago: Marquis Academic Media, 1975]).

CHAPTER 5

Adult and Continuing Education:
Its Professionals

WHO IS AN ADULT AND CONTINUING EDUCATOR?

The question raised by this sectional heading is not an easy one to answer. When one hears the term doctor, lawyer, engineer, schoolteacher, or bus driver, a fairly stable picture of a role and task comes quickly to mind. However, an adult educator can be thought of as a county agent, a teacher who works with illiterate or foreign-born adults, or often as a "what?"

One of the difficulties in describing a professional adult educator is the fact that so many people are now working with adult learners in different capacities, as could be seen from the discussion in Chapter 4. Consequently, one person who considers himself or herself a professional adult educator might have an entirely different kind of position than another person who is considered an educator of adults.

For example, Figure 5.1 lists numerous professional positions held by doctoral graduates from the University of Nebraska's Adult and Continuing Education Department. It should be noted that a variety of agencies, institutional forms, and professional roles are represented. In addition, many adult education positions throughout the United States are filled with capable people who do not have a formal college degree or who have degrees in other than adult education. In addition, many positions as teachers, counselors, and learning resource center personnel are available to bachelor and masters degree holders in adult education. The point in illustrating the range of positions available in adult education is to show to the interested reader that tremendous opportunities do exist. Thus, anyone who finds satisfaction in working with the adult learner can usually obtain full-time employment doing just that.

Because a variety of opportunities in adult and continuing education is available and because so many people have found special satisfaction in working with the adult learner, a goodly share of people working in the field have arrived there "through the back door." This last phrase is an oft-used one in adult education circles to refer to the many people who find themselves professionally responsible for adult learners without having had any training directly related to adult education.

Such a situation has often meant that additional training and knowledge

Assistant to Vice President for University Extension
Director of Administration and Finance in a Community College
Associate Professor, University Graduate Program of Nursing
College Dean
Command Chaplain in the Air Force
Associate State Leader of Cooperative Extension
Senior Vice President in an Insurance Company
Early Childhood Coordinator in a Canadian College
Director of Conferences in a University
Private Consultant in Adult Education
Assistant Director of Continuing Medial Education at a University
Director of Student Services at a Community College
Program Coordinator for Community Services in a Community College
Assistant Professor Agricultural Education in a University
Director of Adult and Continuing Education in a Community College
Television Broadcaster
Director of University Information
Assistant Director of Programs and Conferences at a University
Area Director of Extension for a University
Associated Dean in a University
Director of an Employee Development Unit for the U.S. Soil Conservation
   Service
Extension Area Specialist
Associate State 4-H Leader
Minority Student Counselor at a University
Special Assistant to a University President
Director of Evaluation for a Learning Resource Center
Director of Adult Education at a Foreign University
Dean of Continuing Education at a University

Figure 5.1. Positions Held by Some Doctoral Graduates from the University of Nebraska's Department of Adult and Continuing Education

were acquired through formalized programs or through intensive self-study efforts. Fortunately, as the number enrolled in formal adult education graduate programs and the awareness of adult education opportunities have increased, those professionally trained in adult education have also increased, providing a large corps of people with a good understanding of the adult learner and knowledge of how to develop effective programs for such learners.

The purpose of the next section will be to describe the most common types of roles performed by individuals known as adult and continuing educators. In addition, the particular requisite skills for each type will be included in the discussion.

TYPES OF ADULT AND CONTINUING EDUCATORS

There are various types of roles performed by individuals who consider themselves to be professional adult educators. The variety of roles is increasing as the profession matures. However, there appear to be three fairly distinct categories or types. They will be described in the following subsections, with a fourth subsection added to describe the remaining mixture of positions.

Administrative Roles

One very significant role in organizing and implementing adult education efforts is that of administrator. Whether it be a community college, a learning resource center, a YMCA, or a voluntary agency, someone must administer the programs, be in charge of teacher and student recruitment, work with the board or council, develop a suitable budget, and give the basic program leadership. In addition, most state departments of education have one or more adult education specialists who administer the state ABE programs and who provide general adult education leadership to local communities.

Consequently, adult education administrators must have many of the same skills as any other type of program administrator. A problem to be faced, though, is that adult education is often in a marginal or supporting role, with scarce resources, an evolving "territory," and an ever-changing clientele base. In addition, the adult participant is seldom enrolled in educational programs unless he or she wants to be. This means, therefore, that the adult education administrator must thoroughly understand how to involve the adult student in the learning endeavor, how to design programs based on adult needs, and how to set up learning activities that are based on what is known about how adults learn. Such an understanding must be the basis for program planning, for training teachers, and for coordinating each single effort with a workable whole.

Teaching Roles

By far the largest category of adult educator is that of teacher. These positions range from full-time Adult Basic Education teachers, to teachers of noncredit evening classes such as knitting, oil painting, or wills and estate planning, to vocational teachers in a trade school. However, many adult education teachers do not earn their primary incomes in such roles.

Consequently, one of the problems is how to distinguish between a teacher who simply has the adult as student and a teacher who is trained specifically to facilitate learning for the adult as student. Because the field of adult education is in an evolving stage compared to most other professions, probably the largest share of adult education teachers have had very little specific training related to the adult as learner. Hopefully, as the field matures, as it gains better financial support, and as adult teacher-training programs are more fully developed, this situation can be reversed.

Professorial Roles

Numerous institutions of higher education throughout the United States have either departments of adult and continuing education or at least offer classes, primarily at the graduate level, for prospective adult educators. For example, in 1973, 21 institutions of higher education graduated 146 doctoral students in adult and continuing education.

Those individuals who subsequently undertake an adult education professorial role will typically divide their time between (1) teaching and working with students who are wanting to become adult educators or to become at least acquainted with the field, (2) carrying out research and scholarly pursuits related to adult education as a profession, and (3) carrying out a variety of service activities that attempt to extend the resources of the department and university beyond the campus walls.

Much of the following section will be related to describing several positions or roles emerging in a variety of agencies. Much of the training and preparation required for people in these roles is carried out by professors and graduate departments of adult education.

Miscellaneous Roles

There are several other recognizable roles that do not fall neatly into any of the above three categories. A rapidly developing area of interest, for example, is that of counselor for adult education students. An adult education counselor will no doubt need many of the skills required for any of the other roles described above; in addition, he or she will need to be able to adapt general counseling and testing techniques to adult learners.

Another role somewhat different from the others described to date is that of learning resource center facilitator. Such individuals will need teaching skills, counseling skills, and administrative skills; however, they will also need to be skilled at directing individualized learning, discovering various resources for learning outside the normal classroom setting, and coordinating the learning efforts of several learners progressing at various rates.

Somewhat related to several of the roles already described but still different enough to require explanation is that of the non-traditional "mentor." The recent emergence of and interest in the non-traditional forms of learning has created the need for faculty leadership somewhat different from what has been typical. Mentors work with learners primarily on a one-to-one basis. Such individuals must serve as teachers, helpers, advisors, and counselors, as well as being a contributor to program-planning effort and a developer of learning resources. Such a person will not only need to thoroughly understand how to work with the adult learner, but also how to discover and coordinate a variety of resources for learning that are available in most communities.

A final professional role to be discussed in this section is one that cannot be described easily by a recognizable title. Consequently, for lack of a better title the term "consultant" will be used. Consultants often serve in program-planning, evaluation, or research positions, frequently on a part-time or short-term basis, and increasingly in federally funded projects. A person in a consultant role might also provide leadership for workshops or conferences, serve as in-service training directors for business and industry, or operate in some politically related capacity. Individuals who serve in these roles often have more specialized expertise such as research, educational psychology, or management skills in addition to general adult education skills.

No doubt several types of positions are not covered in the above classifications. Nor do the descriptions cover the many people working in the adult education field as paraprofessional or volunteer leaders. Such individuals perform a variety of important tasks.

TRAINING AND PREPARATION OF ADULT EDUCATORS

As suggested above, there are various ways adult educators are prepared for their roles and responsibilities. These range from graduate degree programs to in-service training activities to self-study efforts. The purpose of this section will be to describe the most common means utilized for the training and preparation of adult education professionals.

Formal Graduate Programs

There is a large number of institutions of higher education in the United States providing graduate training opportunities in adult and continuing education in the form of graduate degrees or areas of specialization. The Appendix at the end of this chapter contains a listing of those institutions. Other institutions are just initiating graduate training in adult education. Consequently, the Appendix should be considered to represent only a partial listing.

It is estimated that through 1973 at least 1,393 doctorates in adult education had been awarded since the first one was granted in 1935. More than half of these have been granted in just the past few years. There is no accurate means for deriving the number of masters degrees in adult education that have been awarded in the United States. It is safe to assume, however, that the number is large and growing.

There has been considerable interest shown in adult education at the bachelors degree level during the seventies. At this time, the author only knows of three programs in adult education at the bachelors degree level being offered by colleges and universities. However, several other institutions have proposals for such programs being considered and many institutions now have undergraduate courses in adult education. Most undergraduate courses are utilized as part of preservice teacher education programs, not only to provide an expanded awareness of all forms of education, but to also provide some beginning skills in working with adults because K–12 teachers are often asked to teach in evening adult education programs or in Adult Basic Education programs. In addition, the emergence of non-traditional degree programs across the United States at the undergraduate level has meant that participants in such programs often receive training which resembles graduate adult education training in many ways.

There is a fairly recognizable pattern to the nature of training received in adult education. One or more courses built around each of the following competency expectations usually serve as a base for the training effort:

Understanding of learning theory as it applies to the adult.
Understanding of the adult personality and adult psychology.
Skill in administering adult education programing efforts.
Skill in planning and evaluating adult education programs.
Understanding of theory emerging and evolving that is related specifically to adult education.
Knowledge of the various philosophical adult education underpinnings.
Knowledge of the history of adult education in the United States.
Understanding of the institutions and forms of adult education.
Knowledge of the societal issues important to adult education.
Ability to carry out research in adult education.

Obviously, doctoral degree expectations will be greater than bachelors or masters degree requirements. Such expectations will usually include greater exposure to the behavioral sciences through course work outside of adult education, practical experience in adult education through internships or practicums, and demonstrations of scholarly abilities through advanced research-related course work, independent research activities, and published materials.

In-Service Training

In-service training in adult education serves an important role because, as was described earlier, so many people find themselves carrying out responsibilities related to working with adults almost accidentally. Consequently, many individuals increase their skills and knowledge through a variety of in-service means.

One very common means of obtaining help in working with the adult learner is through short-term workshops. Often for two or three weeks and typically for graduate credit, these workshops provide a concentrated exposure to some aspect of adult education. The largest share of such workshops is usually concentrated on the improvement of skills, such as in selecting appropriate methods and materials for the adult learner, designing instructional settings for the adults, and developing more effective communication skills in working with the independently inclined adult person.

Another often used means of providing training is through seminars or conferences. The typical time allotment is even shorter than for workshops, usually two or three days. The purpose is often to provide new information or to heighten awareness on such topics as the uniqueness of the adult learner, research findings related to adult education, and new approaches in adult education.

The emergence in the 1960s of special monies and attention to the plight of the disadvantaged or illiterate adult stimulated the Adult Basic Education (ABE) movement. This has resulted in a large corps of ABE teachers and program administrators with little, or at least inadequate, training in, or preparation for, working with the ABE student. Subsequently, the staff development needs for such individuals have been immense.

Consequently, several regional and national projects received special federal funding in the 1960s and early 1970s for purposes of teacher training, primarily for ABE teachers. Reading materials for teachers' self-study, summer workshops, and special graduate training programs were the primary products from these investments. More recently, national and state funding for ABE has begun to be used for more formal staff development programs. Regional and state efforts have included not only workshops and conferences but also mobile educational vans, graduate courses off the college campuses, and special study programs for teachers who are released temporarily from their regular duties.

Various other organizations have discovered the need to employ continuing education concepts in staff development. Business and industrial groups, medical and health care organizations, and such institutions as community colleges have begun in earnest to utilize various training avenues to keep their staffs current or to retrain staffs for work with ever-changing clientele. Consequently, one or more specialists in continuing education are often available in many organizations to administer such continuing education activities.

PROFESSIONAL ASSOCIATIONS IN ADULT EDUCATION

There is a variety of professional associations in the United States that provide support to the training and preparation of professional adult educators. It is suggested that there are three such organizations general enough in nature that they fit some of the needs of almost all adult and continuing educators.

Adult Education Association of the USA (AEA)

The AEA has a current membership base of approximately 3,000 individuals, most of whom reside in the United States. The AEA has a large number of special-interest sections, supports two professional periodicals, publishes a variety of materials, maintains an executive office and elected body to provide leadership to the field, supports a variety of special activities and projects, and sponsors an annual convention that often attracts as many as 1,000 or more participants.

National Association of Public and Continuing Adult Education (NAPCAE)

NAPCAE also has a large membership base from across the United States, numbering nearly 6,000 people. It serves primarily public school adult education teachers and administrators, community college personnel, and state department of education employees, although like the AEA its membership base is quite varied. The association publishes materials, provides special newsletters to its membership, sponsors special activities and programs, maintains an executive office and elected body in order to provide national leadership, and sponsors an annual convention, usually in conjunction with the AEA.

Commission of Professors of Adult Education (CPAE)

The CPAE provides professional affiliation opportunities for those working full and part time as professors or researchers in adult education. The commission is actually a sub-organization of the AEA but carries out independent activities. It currently has approximately 170 full-time members, representing nearly 75 institutions of higher education. CPAE has an elected body of officers, publishes occasional materials, encourages research in adult education, and sponsors an annual convention in conjunction with and preceding the AEA convention.

Various other professional organizations exist to serve more specialized memberships. The National University Extension Association (NUEA), for example, has a large membership base and a prestigious history of service to the many individuals involved with university and college extension activities. The American Society of Training Directors (ASTD) is another organization with a large and varied membership, primarily related, however, to those involved with training efforts in business and industry. Other special areas or groups serviced by adult education–related associations include such groups or organizations as the Cooperative Extension Service, community schools, community colleges, gerontology workers, Adult Basic Education personnel, library workers, evening college personnel, and community developers. Another important organization is the Coalition of Adult Education Organizations, a group that lends some coordinating leadership to the field.

There are also various state and regional adult education associations offering important support to the training of adult and continuing educators. Many states have chapters for most of the national organizations described above. Some states even have developed associations that combine several of the national affiliations into a single state association. The AEA, as one example, has helped in the establishment of various regional AEA associations. Most of these state and regional groups hold annual conventions, publish newsletters and other literature, and sponsor various training activities.

IMPLICATIONS

No doubt many additional means will be required to provide not only graduate or in-service training but also the retraining and upgrading of individuals who have responsibilities in adult and continuing education programs. The shortage of trained adult educators is still a reality, despite the rapid increase in graduate programs. In addition, research efforts in adult education are continuously providing new information that needs to be disseminated to continuing education professionals in a variety of ways. Consequently, the implication of such needs is that much more is required in the way of training.

A related question is what effect does a teacher who possesses little understanding of the adult learner have on the learning environment? Does the disadvantaged adult learner become discouraged if a teacher fails to treat him or her as an adult? Do the self-motivated, mature adults refuse to utilize available services from teachers and organized adult education programs if they sense a child-oriented classroom atmosphere ? These types of questions, largely unanswered, imply that much work still remains related to teacher training and to understanding how to facilitate the learning of every type of adult.

The task is for the field of adult education to become more aware of the adult dimension of regular K–12 school programs. Teachers of children have great potential for cooperation with the adult education field. Thus, it behooves adult educators to work more closely with teacher education institutions to insure that teacher graduates have the skills to work with parents, to work with community leaders, to teach adults, and to help children truly become equipped with learning skills that will facilitate their becoming lifelong learners.

One final implication to be drawn here is related to the future type of adult educator that appears to be needed because of the various change and growth factors suggested in this chapter. Future adult educators will certainly need to be skilled at solving various kinds of problems, especially the many problems that emerge because of growth and societal change. Adult education leaders frequently will need to be more social-action or change-agent oriented if they are to help adults become better equipped to solve various societal problems. Chapter 8 will contain more discussion pertaining to the future and the role of adult education.

SOME DEFINITIONS*

Adult Basic Education teacher—A facilitator of learning for adult students who typically possess less than an eighth-grade level of education. Individualized learning, small-group work, and learning resource center materials are often facilitated by the ABE teacher.

* The terms defined are frequently utilized interchangeably in describing an adult educator.

Adult and continuing educator—An educational agent who may, in dealing with an adult client, carry out one or more of the following tasks in relation to learning activities: planning, initiating, administering, teaching, and evaluating.

Change agent—An individual who designs and/or directs educational activities for purposes of bringing about or influencing some type of change.

Facilitator—An individual who acts in a catalytic manner to make learning activity possible and learning probable.

Mentor—Utilized primarily with non-traditional education programs, the term refers to a person who works as an educational facilitator with a learner, frequently on a one-to-one basis.

Resource person—An individual whose experiences and knowledge are the bases for information or direction sought by an adult learner.

STUDY STIMULATORS

1. What are the various terms utilized in your community or state to describe a person who works in an educational capacity with adults?
2. What kinds of training (content, duration, frequency) should a person seek who suddenly finds himself or herself working with adults but who has had no prior training or experience in adult education?
3. Should there be more bachelor degree training programs in adult and continuing education? Why?
4. What kinds of training should be offered to volunteer adult education leaders? To paraprofessional adult educators?
5. Should K–12 teachers in training at the undergraduate level receive any exposure to adult education?
6. Determine what opportunities exist in your community in the way of graduate, undergraduate, or in-service training related to adult education.
7. Are there any professional adult education associations in your state? Analyze the type of members each different association attracts.
8. What will be some future training needs of existing professional adult educators as the American adults becomes more "lifelong learning" in nature?

SELECTED BIBLIOGRAPHY

APPS, JEROLD W. "Tomorrow's Adult Educator—Some Thoughts and Questions," *Adult Education*, 22, No. 3 (Spring 1972), pp. 218–26. The author describes some competencies he perceives will be needed in the future by adult educators. Orientations to people, problems, and change are some of the needs discussed.

BOYD, ROBERT D. "New Designs for Adult Education Doctoral Programs," *Adult Education*, 19, No. 3 (Spring 1969), pp. 186–96. The author describes some components to be considered in developing graduate adult education programs.

CARLSON, ROBERT A. "Professional Leadership vs. the Educational Service Station Approach: An Historical Appraisal," *Adult Education*, 22, No. 4 (Summer 1972), pp. 291–99. The author makes a case based on historical study that a struggle over priorities in leadership development is rapidly approaching in adult education.

DICKINSON, GARY, and RUBIDGE, NICHOLAS A. "Testing Knowledge About Adult Education," *Adult Education*, 23, No. 4 (Summer 1973), pp. 283–97. The authors present an instrument they developed to test knowledge about adult education possessed by adult education graduate students.

DOUGLAH, MOHAMMAD A, and MOSS, GWENNA M. "Adult Education as a Field of Study and Its Implications," *Adult Education*, 19, No. 2 (Winter 1969), pp. 127–34. The authors describe the role of graduate programs in the development of adult education. Objectives of graduate study, competencies, and professional roles are also discussed.

FARMER, JAMES A., JR. "Impact of 'Lifelong Learning' on the Professionalization of Adult Education," *Journal of Research and Development in Education*, 7, No. 4 (Summer 1974), pp. 57–67. The author describes his views on professionalization and discusses the question of whether adult education is a profession. He also presents some challenges to the professional attempting to operate in a lifelong learning environment.

KNOX, ALAN B. *Development of Adult Education Graduate Programs*. Washington, D.C.: Adult Education Association of the USA, 1973. 64 pages. This volume contains a wealth of information on the status of graduate programs in adult education across the United States. It also suggests ways of attracting students, building support, and involving students.

From other chapters:

Chapter 2. Liveright

Chapter 3. Tough

Chapter 4.Grabowski and Glenn

Jensen et al.

Marquis Academic Media

APPENDIX

Institutions of Higher Education with Graduate Adult Education Opportunities

Alabama

Alabama A & M University

Alabama State University

Auburn University

Tuskegee Institute

Arizona

Arizona State University

University of Arizona

Arkansas

University of Arkansas

California

United States International University

University of California—Berkeley

University of California—Los Angeles

University of Southern California

Colorado

Colorado State University

Connecticut

University of Connecticut

District of Columbia

Federal City College

George Washington University

Howard University

Florida

Florida A & M University

Florida Atlantic University

Florida International University

Florida State University

University of South Florida

Georgia
Georgia Southern College
University of Georgia
West Georgia College

Illinois
Northern Illinois University
University of Chicago
University of Illinois

Indiana
Ball State University
Indiana University

Iowa
Iowa State University
University of Iowa

Kansas
Kansas State University

Louisiana
Louisiana State University

Maine
University of Maine—Orono
University of Maine—
Portland/Gorham

Maryland
University of Maryland

Massachusetts
Boston University
Worcester State College

Michigan
Michigan State University
University of Michigan

Minnesota
Morehead State University
University of Minnesota

Mississippi
Jackson State University
Mississippi State University

Missouri
University of Missouri—Columbia
University of Missouri—Kansas City

Nebraska
University of Nebraska

New Jersey
Montclair State College
Rutgers University

New York
City University of New York
Columbia University
Cornell University
State University of New York—
Albany
State University of New York—
Buffalo
Syracuse University

North Carolina
North Carolina State University
University of North Carolina

Ohio
Ohio State University

Oregon
Oregon State University

Pennsylvania
Indiana University of Pennsylvania
Pennsylvania State University
Temple University

Rhode Island
Rhode Island College
University of Rhode Island

South Carolina
South Carolina State College
University of South Carolina

Tennessee
Memphis State University
University of Tennessee

Texas
Incarnate Word College
North Texas State University
Texas A & M University

Utah
University of Utah

Vermont
University of Vermont

Virginia
Virginia Commonwealth University
Virginia Polytechnic Institute & S.U.

Wisconsin
University of Wisconsin—Madison
University of Wisconsin—Milwaukee

Wyoming
University of Wyoming

CHAPTER 6

The Community and Adult Education

THE COMMUNITY AS A SETTING FOR ADULT EDUCATION

Knowing your community, the different ways in which a community is conceptualized, and the dynamics of change acting constantly on the American community are crucial to maintaining viability as an educator or even as an effective citizen. In addition, the community is the natural setting for most adult and continuing education programs (see Chapter 4). Thus, the purpose of this section is to facilitate for the reader an understanding of the concept of community and its relationship to people so that future problem solving through education may be made more effective.

Understanding Community

The obvious question in an attempt to understand the concept of community is simply what is a community? Unfortunately, a simple answer is impossible to give because the term has been defined in numerous ways, is conceptualized in so many different ways by residents of communities, and is constantly changing in meaning because communities themselves continuously evolve.

The term "community" is derived from the Latin *communis*, meaning a fellowship of man. Thus, the term came to mean fellow townsmen, a term similar in scope to the association most people make now to a local town or neighborhood. For purposes of this chapter, the term community refers to a geographical unit of people organized in such a manner that the fulfillment of normal, daily living needs are met. For many people such needs are fulfilled in the neighborhood or small town setting. However, some people would say that their natural home base was a large urban center and this would be their community setting.

Regardless of the actual setting or the size of the community, most individuals have two different kinds of pulls on them that affect their relationship to others.[1] One kind of pull is vertical in nature. By that it is meant that a person might live in Buffalo, New York, but have affiliatory relationships to organizations, associations, and individuals outside the community (belonging to a

1. Extended discussions of the vertical and horizontal relationships within the community setting can be found in the sources by Hiemstra (see Chapter 2) and by Warren cited at the end of this chapter.

professional educational organization, for example, at the national level) that tend to draw allegiances, time of residence, and resources away.

The second kind of pull or relationship can be called horizontal in nature, or within the community. In other words, each person is affiliated with many people, groups, and organizations in the same community he or she calls home. Take the Buffalo, New York, example again: The same person mentioned before will probably belong to a local educational association, have friends and relatives, and associate with various kinds of groups all located within a few miles of the actual place of residence. It is the horizontal direction of relationships that is most crucial in creating a personal sense of community.

The dynamic state of modern society, due to advancing technology and constant social change, is continuously imposing new strains on daily living. One may hold a personal value judgment on whether constant change is good or bad, but the vertical pulls are becoming increasingly more apparent as we are urged to become a world society. Thus, one premise underlying this chapter, and indeed, every chapter, is that adult education as a vital force in lifelong learning can be a means of strengthening the horizontal relationships of a person within his or her community and thereby facilitate a heightened sense of community.

There is evidence that a renewed sense of community is being developed in many parts of the United States. For example, the newspapers frequently report that people are rallying around various community issues such as forced busing, declining school enrollments, or community improvement projects. Any such issues will be judged bad by some and good by others, but the community or neighborhood can be seen as the setting for the activity. Additional evidence can be found in what has been dubbed by some as the "back-to-earth" movement. Whether it is a rebellion against bigness or simply a desire to be more self-sufficient, growing numbers of individuals are returning to more rural or smaller settings as their community base.

Another aspect of the local community as a setting for adult education is the fact that the relationship of the community to education for adults is fairly direct. Each person is primarily the product of his or her community. A person receives vocational retraining, for example, as the local job conditions demand it. In addition, educational access to an individual is most effectively gained through local channels of communication. Thus, adult education programs and activities are carried out in local schools or community colleges, through local agencies or organizations, and by using forms of media with which the person is acquainted.

Finally, the local community is a logical setting for adult and continuing education that is aimed at helping people fulfill citizenship roles and solve their own unique community problems. More discussion on involving people in community activities will be contained in the remainder of the chapter.

The Community Education Movement

The community education movement is an important one for American education. It has the potential of bringing about considerable change to traditional K–12 programs and has already changed significantly many communities in the United States and other countries. Perhaps even more important is the potential that community education has in involving adults with educational activities.

The history of community education is quite long in the United States. The Highlander Folk School in Tennessee, for example, has been in existence since the 1930s. Richard Poston involved persons in solving community problems in the 1930s and 1940s in Montana. The Ogdens worked with small communities in Virginia during the 1940s. A community education project using combined mass media was operated by the San Bernardino Valley College in California during the 1950s. The Biddles helped to develop local community initiative in the Appalachians during the 1950s and early 1960s. The University of Nebraska's Teachers College received financial assistance from the Carnegie Foundation to develop some model community education programs in several Nebraska communities during the late 1950s and early 1960s.

Perhaps the largest single contributor to the current community education interest has been the Flint, Michigan, community school program. Facilitated by financial grants from the Mott Foundation, the Flint Public Schools began in 1935 to utilize more fully school facilities and resources of the community for educating both adults and youth. Adult and extended youth education programs, the use of the school as a community center, the involvement of neighborhood residents in planning and implementing programs, and the use of trained community and adult education specialists in local schools are normal features of the community school.

Currently, the community school or community education idea is receiving increasing attention throughout the United States and in other countries. Approximately 700 school districts, 5,000 different neighborhood schools, and up to 20 million citizens have been reached by community education activities. Many of those involved are engaging in a variety of adult education activities including such programs as Adult Basic Education, adult high school, adult vocational training, arts and crafts training, community lectures and discussion, academic credit courses, personal growth opportunities, recreation and physical fitness, senior citizen activities, and technical or professional upgrading.

Several states have legislation that provides financial support to local communities for purposes of initiating and operating community education programs. In addition, federal legislation has been enacted that will provide monies to states for local school districts to employ community school coordinators, for state-level programing assistance, and for the preparation and training of community education specialists. At the time this chapter is being written monies have yet to be appropriated but most educators are optimistic that the support soon will be available.

The Mott Foundation has also been instrumental in supporting the training of professional educators so that they may gain knowledge and experience in community education. Nearly 400 Mott Fellows, as they were called, were trained through the Mott Inter-University Clinical Preparation Program for Community Education.[2] Many of these individuals are in positions of leadership in community and adult education throughout the United States. A related training program now is being implemented on a regional basis, although various short-term training opportunities still exist through the Flint Center.

In conjunction with and follow-up to the above program, regional centers for community education have been established throughout the United States. Cooperating centers now exist in 46 states and the District of Columbia and involve 57 universities and 21 other organizations. Each center provides training opportunities for educational leaders interested in community and adult education, offers consultative services to local communities in understanding and initiating community education programs, and provides some funding assistance to selected communities. Many of the centers are also in the process of developing cooperative programs with junior and community colleges, with county boards of education, and with state departments of education.

The community education movement has received important contributions from a variety of institutions, agencies, and community centers in addition to those of the public schools and the cooperating universities. Perhaps one of the most important of these institutions has been the community and junior college. Almost every citizen in the United States has access to a community college campus or at least some community college outreach programs. Through their community service programs, the colleges provide various kinds of adult education programs, coordinate community education programs, and generally attempt to meet the educational needs of citizens not already met through other college or public school programs. The community college has the potential of being the most likely institution in the future to coordinate the various community and adult education opportunities available in an area.

Community Development and Adult Education

The adult educator has been involved with the notion of using educational processes in the development of communities for some time. A noted adult

2. The author was a Mott Fellow in 1967–68. Academic training in adult and community education, experience in a variety of community schools, adult education, and community activities, and discussion with a variety of educational leaders were included in the training year.

educator put it in the following terms: ". . . the adult educator will say that the community is a teacher or developer of the people who live there. At the same time it should be one of the people's obligations to help the community become a better teacher and, in the process of doing so, themselves become better educated."[3]

Community development can be defined as the educational facilitation of an interaction between a community and its residents for purposes of an improvement of both. Thus, the change in the community, the solution of crucial problems, and the corresponding development of leadership are results of the community development process that go beyond what typically is a part of community education. However, as community education programs move beyond the neighborhood school to the activation of a variety of available resources for education and the solution of problems, they will become community development activities.

Like the community education movement, community development activities have been ongoing in various forms for many years in the United States. The Cooperative Extension Service at the county level, social welfare programs, community councils, and the various types of community organizations involved in supporting local self-help or voluntary agencies all have had, as working goals, involving the local citizen in the solution of local problems.

The involvement of the community resident in a solution of problems is a crucial aspect within the adult educator's view of the community development process. The following steps or phases of activity summarize the common elements of a self-help process:

1. Analysis of the problem situation—by either concerned citizens or a change agent.
2. The setting of goals, objectives, and priorities aimed at a solution of the problem or problems.
3. An assessment of the commitment to proceed.
4. Planning and organizing the activities necessary to meet the established goals.
5. Carrying out the planned activities.
6. Evaluating the activities in light of the goals and the initial problem assessment.

The activities described above will not fit exactly all the problem-solving efforts in a community development situation, nor will they always be carried out in the same sequence or to the extent shown. However, they do describe a procedure whereby community residents can be involved in a variety of learning activities in order to solve problems. The role adult educators play in such endeavors will be examined in the next section.

3. Howard Y. McClusky, "Community Development," in the 1960 *Handbook of Adult Education in the United States*, edited by Malcolm Knowles (Washington, D.C.: Adult Education Association of the USA, 1960), p. 416.

Adult Education's Role in the Community

Adult and continuing educators can and usually do play an important role in the community setting. Whether it is from an institutional or agency base or as a private individual, the skills possessed by adult educators can be used in many important ways. For example, facilitating a teaching and learning environment for adults and involving the adult in learning activities are crucial to a community in this era of rapid change. In addition, the increasing interest in lifelong learning because of the change and other factors described in Chapter 1 will create even new demands on the adult educator.

One important role for the adult educator at the community level is understanding people and their problems. Thus, the assessment of needs through community surveys or studies, through advisory councils, by personal observation, by discussions with community leaders and through a multitude of other techniques is a necessary element in the development of adult and continuing education programs or the facilitation of a community development project.

Many needs-assessment activities are based on a concept discussed throughout this chapter—that of involving people in priority setting and problem solving. When recognized problems become a basis for program development, community support and the ultimate success of the efforts are more likely occurrences.

The adult educator also has a responsibility to establish a teaching and learning climate that will maximize the learning and involvement that takes place. Such a process includes facilitating the needs-assessment activities described above, making available various resources for learning, utilizing a person's community experiences as a basis for learning, and providing facilitating expertise as it is necessary. Additional discussion on the teaching and learning theory that has evolved in the adult and continuing education field is contained in Chapter 7.

A tremendous need exists in most communities throughout the United States for the various agencies and organizations sponsoring educational programs to cooperate on such endeavors so that overlap and competition can be minimized and the use of resources can be maximized. Thus, the adult and continuing educator has an important role to play in coordinating such activities as the use of expensive educational buildings, in determining what audiences can be served best by each agency, by ascertaining the educational and training areas of highest priority, and by making information on educational opportunities available to community residents. In addition, a coordinated effort in a community implies that problem-solving efforts will be undertaken by residents representing various walks of life; it also means that educational decisions and many times other kinds of decisions are made by a representative body of individuals and that such information is disseminated throughout the community.

Unfortunately, the coordinating role has not been fulfilled very successfully by adult educators or anyone else in most communities. The horizontal relationships described earlier in this chapter are frequently weak or not established. For example, governmental bodies establish laws or priorities that affect educational institutions but educators, or affected parents, are seldom consulted. A community college may offer several of the same adult education courses offered by a recreation department or YWCA and all the courses experience low enrollments. Educators at the K–12 level develop a new curricular approach to incorporating career education opportunities into the regular offerings without consulting parents or business and industry representatives.

There are several exemplary coordination efforts that have been tried or are being tried by adult educators in various communities. Some communities have established a community council of representatives from various adult education agencies which meets regularly for purposes of sharing programing ideas, establishing common calendars, and finding new ways of working together. In Chicago, the "Learning Exchange" has established a telephone referral service to coordinate adult education needs with adult education resources at the local citizen level. Adult educators in several small communities have been instrumental in developing and maintaining a community guide of educational and societal programs for use by all individuals working in some way with human services. Such efforts and the many others being tried are helping adult educators learn how to fulfill the coordination role.

Another need in many communities, especially smaller ones, is for some central place where various community and educational activities can take place. Adult and community educators have been able to establish the community school as such a site in many communities. Some communities have established the YMCA or YWCA, a church, or some other facility as a central gathering spot. A role remaining for adult and community educators is the development of such sites in many additional communities.

The linking of the home, the school, and the community is still another task with which adult educators need to deal. Involving residents in self-determination efforts, designing effective parent education programs, and keeping a close contact between educators and family members or community leaders are some of the means being employed to meet such a need. No doubt, more can be accomplished, but the growing awareness of education as a lifelong endeavor and the development of such programs as the community school will continue to strengthen the linking of people and their communities.

A final role to be highlighted here is the continuous need for the development of community leadership. For example, many activities of a human service nature in a community operate partially or fully through volunteer leaders. Another related need is for individuals willing and capable of undertaking political and civic responsibilities. Consequently, adult educators have a responsibility to train existing leaders and to find ways of continuously developing new community leaders.

Obviously there are various ongoing roles and tasks performed by adult and continuing educators that were not even mentioned here. The operation of adult education agency programs and the teaching of adult education classes are very important to the vitality of almost every community. The successful fulfillment of such roles, all of those described above, and many more just beginning to evolve or not yet even thought of will be crucial as the notion of lifelong learning becomes a societal reality. In addition, the suggestion of an entirely new role for adult educators and community educators is the basis for the next section.

ACTIVATING THE EDUCATIVE COMMUNITY

The idea of an educative community, or that community in which all available resources for learning are made available to its citizens, is not yet a reality in the United States. The idea of the educative community is similar to what has been labeled before as the "learning society,"[4] or perhaps, even the ancient Greek society aim of utilizing the total society or culture to bring each citizen to his or her fullest development as an individual through education. Although the American society does not fully employ all resources for learning, the lifelong learning movement will soon necessitate such a circumstance.

The use of the total community for learning assumes that most people, organizations, and agencies have a potential and capacity for being a part of the educational process. Thus, in addition to the normal education of youth through a formal school setting, educators in the educative community will need to assume the responsibility of identifying potential resources for education and facilitating their utilization by people of all ages.

Through the visualization of the multitude of resources as potential teachers or learning means, a whole new set of roles for educators and community citizens becomes possible: Teachers learn to supplement K–12 education with visits to community sites, parents can supplement their children's education through the use of various community resources, community parks or open areas become sites to study nature or ecology, church leaders provide education to people of all ages in the area of human relationships, and potential community leaders develop their skills of helping others by specific teaching endeavors in a school classroom. Examples of this nature are limited only by the imaginations or willingness of community residents and educational leaders.

Activation of the educative community will necessitate that educators, parents, and other citizens learn a great deal more about the communities in

4. Robert M. Hutchins, *The Learning Society* (New York: Frederick A. Praeger, 1968).

which they reside. More knowledge about a community and its potential resources for learning can be obtained by personal interviews, mail-out survey forms, the compilation of a directory of existing agencies and their services, and the formation of community task forces whose functions include determining educational resources and helping community residents become aware of such resources.

A brief description of two such activating projects will be described here. A more extended discussion of the projects can be found in the journal article by the author on activating the educative community cited at the end of the chapter.

One project centered around the inclusion of career education activities in the curriculum of an elementary school. A group of elementary teachers became familiar with the idea of an educative community and worked during a summer to identify a series of potential learning resources throughout the community. Individuals willing to make a presentation in the classroom about their careers were identified. Sites where individuals in various careers could be observed were identified for later visitation. Other career areas were depicted by teacher-made video-tapes, through secured films or tape/slide sets, or through teacher-made audiovisual aids. In addition, some of the teachers made curricular guide booklets with suggestions on how to utilize the various resources in conjunction with regular subject areas.

During the following school year and since that time, various of the identified or developed resources have been utilized in the elementary grades. Whether or not the educational process has improved or even if a greater knowledge of career opportunities was sustained has not been ascertained yet in this particular project. However, one thing is clear from the experiences of these teachers—a variety of potential resources for learning existed in this one community.

The second project is an ongoing one in the state of Nebraska. A group of graduate students in adult and continuing education at the University of Nebraska each year identify various community agencies, groups, or individuals with a potential for the education of others who are not overtly engaged in providing for learning. After consultation with the organization or agency, the students help to develop a plan whereby some learning service can be made available.

A variety of projects have been completed to date and many have become ongoing services. For example, several medically related professionals now include periodically some health education literature in their monthly statements. A major bank includes information on adult and continuing education opportunities in its monthly statements. A small farm community's grain elevator manager maintains an updated bulletin board display of articles, brochures, and other information related to crop management. The possibilities are limitless and the acceptance by the cooperating people or agencies has been gratifying, suggesting that the activation of the educative community may not be very difficult or very expensive.

IMPLICATIONS FOR THE FIELD OF EDUCATION

The discussion presented throughout the chapter suggests that several new roles for educators are needed or possible if education is to be made more available on a community-wide basis. For example, K–12 teachers should become knowledgeable regarding an understanding of the community, its power structure, and its resources. Skills will be needed on how to study a community, how to coordinate school activities with adult education programs, and how to work more closely with parents. In addition, the educational activities of a teacher may need to include occasional visits to homes, the administering of needs-assessment projects, or an involvement with educational programs outside the school setting. Several of the above activities will need to become accepted endeavors during the regular working day.

A continued growth of community education and community school programs throughout the United States will also necessitate that each school official become familiar with the related philosophy and programing possibilities inherent in the community education movement. Enriching the school curriculum with extended school activities and learning to relate to the whole child are examples of such a philosophy. Various books and films cited at the conclusion of the chapter describe the community education concepts.

Perhaps one of the most crucial implications is for educators to help integrate education into the entire life of the community. This must include identifying potential educational resources and planning for their use, helping interested citizens learn how to use the resources, and adjusting school or higher education curriculum to maximize the learning potential of community experiences. The two activating examples described in the previous section only begin to scratch the surface of what can be done at the adult level.

Another task for educators is helping to develop a more extended use of school facilities by people of all ages. Keeping central buildings open more hours each year, utilizing athletic and auditorium facilities more extensively, creating a community center facility, and involving K–12 teachers in adult education activities are some of the possibilities already being implemented in many communities. Additional uses only need to be experimented with by interested school officials.

Implied, too, by the information presented in this chapter are new roles for parents. It should be possible in most communities for parents to supplement and reinforce in the home the education taking place in each school by using community resources. In some cases there are also responsibilities that could be undertaken by parents directly in the schools. In addition, because the first few years of a person's life are so important to later development, important learning skills and positive attitudes toward education could no doubt be more effectively developed in the home if parents were more knowledgeable and positive about learning. Consequently, effective parent education and leadership training programs are needed in the educative community.

Another implication, especially vital in view of the lifelong learning information, is for K–12 and college educators to become more aware of the adult and continuing education field. Such an awareness should include being knowledgeable of the various adult education opportunities and agencies in each community, developing a close working relationship with adult education colleagues, and even working as a part-time teacher of adult education.[5] In addition, each K–12 educator should be able to utilize existing adult and higher education resources for purposes of continuing their own growth and development.

There are also several implications that should be considered by schools of education and teachers colleges in the United States. For example, there is a need for university personnel to understand community theory in order to help teachers in training learn how to work more effectively at the community level. Consequently, an exposure of students to community theory, the provision of off-campus experiences in community activities, and the development of activating skills such as those suggested in this chapter are some of the activities that could be facilitated. Experienced teachers would no doubt benefit from similar learning opportunities if they could be made available through in-service or extension education opportunities.

Administrators of K–12 education, too, will need to support and become involved with the various activities described above. Thus, schools of education will need to facilitate related education for administrators in training and for administrators already on the job.

Various additional roles by colleges and universities are possible. University experts working on special community problems or with special audiences, helping educators at the community level learn how to utilize various nontraditional approaches to education, and carrying out the research necessary to solve various community problems are only some of the possible roles. It is hoped that higher education personnel and K–12 educators will accept the challenges presented by a wider use of the community in lifelong learning.

SOME DEFINITIONS

Change agent—Persons or agency representatives who instigate purposeful social action activities.

Community—The organization of various social activities and units in such a manner that the daily living of a certain set of people is facilitated.

Community education—This can be thought of as a way of viewing education in the

5. The article cited at the end of the chapter by O'Hanlin and Hiemstra suggests several additional roles the educator could consider undertaking at the community level.

locality setting, a means by which people, their problems, and community resources are central to designing an educational program. The traditional role of the school is thereby expanded to one of identifying needs, problems, and concerns of the community and then assisting in the development and utilization of programs toward improving the entire community.

Community school—A site serving as a center for community education. Sometimes referred to as the "lighted school house," the community school attempts to facilitate education to all groups of people at all times of the day and year.

Educative community—That community which is a learning laboratory in its totality.

Horizontal relationships—The association of one individual to another individual within the same locality such as a neighborhood or a city.

Vertical relationships—The association of an individual to another individual or to a group based primarily on group membership affiliation. The affiliation usually includes membership outside of the locality setting.

STUDY STIMULATORS

1. Randomly select a half dozen residents from your community. Ask each person to define in his or her own words the term "community." Note the differences and the similarities.
2. Analyze the various horizontal and vertical pulls on yourself or someone else you can interview. How would one go about strengthening his or her horizontal relationships in a community?
3. Determine how the neighborhood school buildings in your community are being utilized for other than K–12 activities.
4. What sort of legislation does your state have pertaining to community schools or community education? What amount of financial support is provided at the local level from state and national sources for community education?
5. Assume that you are new to a community and would like to be instrumental in establishing viable adult education activities. How would you go about determining the educational needs and interests of the residents?
6. Taking the situation established in Number 5 above, how would you go about facilitating the coordination of existing educational activities?
7. Determine if any sort of community guide booklet on available human services exists in your community. If one does not exist or if it does not contain information pertaining to education programs, you may wish to facilitate the development of such material.
8. What type of community centers exist in your community? Assess whether or not educational activities for adults take place in the centers.
9. Design and implement a project to activate the educative community. Use as a guide the two examples described earlier in the chapter but remember that the potential in almost every community is limitless.

SELECTED BIBLIOGRAPHY

Books and Articles

BIDDLE, WILLIAM W., and BIDDLE, LOUREIDE J. *The Community Development Process: The Rediscovery of Local Initiative.* New York: Holt, Rinehart, & Winston,

1965. 334 pages. Index. Bibliography. Appendixes. The authors are guided by the philosophy that community development is essentially human development. They identify the means by which citizens in the small towns and urban neighborhoods of America can be encouraged to take action in an attempt to improve their local situation and to create or reaffirm a sense of community.

HIEMSTRA, ROGER. "Community Adult Education in Lifelong Learning," *Journal of Research and Development in Education*, 7, No. 4 (Summer 1974), pp. 34–44. This article describes the relationship of the community to adult education in light of the lifelong learning movement.

————. "Educating Parents in the Use of the Community," *Adult Leadership*, 23, No. 3 (September 1974), pp. 85–88. The author describes a variety of ways whereby parents could be assisted to play a larger role in the education of their children. Learning how to utilize a variety of community resources for education is the theme.

————. "The Educative Community in Action," *Adult Leadership*, 24, No. 3 (November 1975), pp. 82–85. The author describes how various resources in a community may be used in new ways for adult education.

————. "Rejuvenation of Community Ed in Nebraska," *Community Education Journal*, 3, No. 5 (September 1973), pp. 32–33. The article contains a description of Nebraska's community education project in the 1950s and 1960s and the new efforts in the 1970s.

IRWIN, MARTHA, and RUSSELL, WILMA. *The Community Is the Classroom*. Midland, Mich.: Pendell Publishing Company, 1971. 131 pages. Bibliography. The authors have documented examples and experiences that show the possibilities of utilizing the community as an open classroom. Chapters center on developing community-centered curricula. Teachers, administrators, and concerned parents are the proposed audiences for the book.

KERENSKY, VASIL M., and MELBY, ERNEST O. *Education II—The Social Imperative*. Midland, Mich.: Pendell Publishing Company, 1971. 192 pages. Bibliography. Centering on the challenges of education in the urban community and with the disadvantaged, the authors propose that education for all people is feasible and possible, provided we better utilize the resources and knowledge already available. The authors also examine the utilization of various community resources.

MCMAHON, ERNEST E. *Needs—of People and Their Communities—and the Adult Educator*. Washington, D.C.: Adult Education Association of the USA, 1970. 50 pages. Bibliography. This booklet is designed as a text for community workers. It suggests how the needs of people can be assessed and how to utilize the acquired information in program planning. An important part of the booklet is an extensive annotated bibliography of many articles and books related to needs assessment and program planning.

MINZEY, JACK D, and LeTARTE, CLYDE. *Community Education: From Program to Process*. Midland, Mich.: Pendell Publishing Company, 1972. 275 pages. The authors have developed an introduction to designing and implementing community education programs. Staffing, budgeting, facility needs, and the planning are some of the topics covered.

O'HANLIN, JAMES, and HIEMSTRA, ROGER. "The Educator as Community Resource," *Contemporary Education*, 46, No. 2 (Winter, 1975), pp. 127–30. The authors urge educators to play a bigger role in communities and to utilize their various educational skills in such activities as problem solving, program planning, and in-service training outside of the school setting.

Powers, Ronald C. *Identifying the Community Power Structure.* North Central Regional Extension Publication No. 19, NCRS-5 Leadership Series No. 2. Ames, Iowa: Iowa State University, Cooperative Extension Service, Soc. 18, 1965. 11 pages. Selected bibliography. This bulletin draws upon the research and experience of sociologists in presenting a technique for the identification of key influentials or power figures in a community. It also provides some discussion of the role community power figures play in decision making.

Seay, Maurice, and Associates. *Community Education: A Developing Concept.* Midland, Mich.: Pendell Publishing Company, 1974. 424 pages. Bibliography. Name and subject indexes. The various authors have compiled a wealth of information on the community education concept. Leadership training, administrative structures, advisory councils, and relationships with other organizations are some topics covered.

Warren, Roland L. *The Community in America.* Chicago: Rand McNally, 1963. 306 pages. Author and subject indexes. It is the thesis of the book that changes in community living include an increasing orientation of local organizations and individuals toward extra-community systems. The phenomenon has resulted in a corresponding decline in community cohesion and autonomy. Suggested are some community action models for dealing with the changes.

Other Sources:

Ogden, Jean, and Ogden, Jess. *These Things We Tried.* Charlottesville, Va.: Extension Division, University of Virginia, 1947.

Poston, Richard W. *Small Town Renaissance.* New York: Harper & Brothers, 1950.

Additional sources can be found referenced in earlier chapters:

    Chapter 2. Hiemstra   Chapter 4. Knowles, 1960

Periodicals

Community Education Journal. Issues were published six times per year. Pendell Company, Midland, Mich. The journal stopped publication in 1974 but back issues contain useful information on the community education movement.

Community Development. Journal of the Community Development Society, published biannually, Columbia, Mo. A variety of articles appear related to the involvement of local citizens in community and educational problem solving.

Films*

To Touch a Child, Thursday's Child, and *A Sense of Community.* All these films are related to the community education movement.

* The films are available through the Mott Programs, Flint, Michigan.

CHAPTER 7

Theoretical Bases and Research
in Adult Education

INTRODUCTION

Is there a unique theory of, or theory for, adult and continuing education? That question is a difficult one to answer; it will not be fully answered in this chapter. The uniqueness of adult education and the adult learner has been discussed, described, and researched for many years, especially by those who consider themselves to be adult education professionals. Some of the resulting information will be summarized in this chapter.

Many of the factors prompting the long and continuous argument over the uniqueness of adult and continuing education have stemmed from the marginal status given adult educators by other educators or by professionals in related disciplines. For example, most of the past educational research and theory-building has been concentrated on youth, on curriculum design needs for K–12 schools and for colleges, and on the leadership skills needed to teach and administer youth-related education.

However, as suggested in Chapter 1, the many forces necessitating lifelong learning by most people have also resulted in expanded research in adult education, a rapidly increasing body of related literature, and increased attention to adult education as a unique field of endeavor. As knowledge about the adult learner and the design or operation of programs for the adult has accumulated through research and experience, those individuals who think of themselves as adult educators have been able to move away from a marginal status to one of professionalism. Such a movement has done much to promote the research, writing, and commitment necessary to develop a theory base for adult education.

Whether or not adult education is a discipline, a field of endeavor, or a profession will not be argued here. The reader is referred to several of the references cited at the end of the chapter for more discussion on such topics. However, what will be presented in this chapter is information, emerging theory, and theory borrowed from other disciplines that pertain specifically to educational programing for the adult as student.

It should be obvious that there are several limitations in attempting to describe through one chapter the relevant research and theory for a field of study. Some readers will find little new information and would wish for more synthesis and a deeper probing regarding what is known about adult education. Other readers will find too much new information to digest with one reading. In addition, a decision was made not to footnote each separate research finding, research report, or book used so that the size of the chapter could remain relatively similar to the other chapters. Thus, it is the hope of the author that the information will be seen as a basic reference point and that additional study of the various references cited at the end of the chapter and other material will be carried out.

Why Have a Theory?

A person who relates to other people in some manner requires or works from theoretical bases applicable to the problems being faced. Frequently, such bases cannot be verbalized or are not recognized; however, personal values, a philosophy of dealing with others, and procedural techniques stem in some manner from theory and practice. The adult teacher must know something about a teaching and learning process; an adult education administrator must know something about leadership; an adult counselor must know something about psychology.

Adult educators have at least one major goal in common with other educators and with many professionals from various social science areas—the utilization of the most effective organizational forms and interaction processes available for supplying educational services to people with learning needs. The differences in approaches to solving educational problems or to meeting known learning needs will usually stem from known differences in the person to be served.

Thus, information presented in this chapter will be based primarily on research about the adult person as opposed to youth. However, it should be obvious that generalizations about the adult learner are nearly impossible because of the various ages, educational backgrounds, and socioeconomic levels. Many of the findings or assumed theoretical bases presented in the next two major sections have not been verified with every different category of adult learner. Nor is there justification in most instances for suggesting that the information pertains exclusively to the adult person, as opposed to the K–12 or college age student. What is found to be a good teaching-learning technique for an older adult, for example, frequently can be very effective with a young adult or a child.

In addition, a considerable amount of the theoretical framework that supports any educator is borrowed and reformulated from a variety of disciplines. As Figure 7.1 shows, the adult educator makes use of knowledge from several sources, such as general educational theory and theory from a variety of the social sciences. The overlapping areas among the three circles represent how theory from one area also fits or is reformulated for use in another area, Some of the primary contributions various other disciplines have made to the

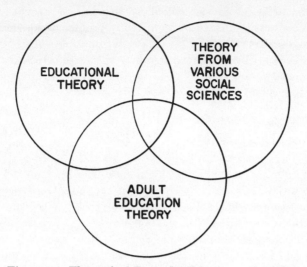

Figure 7.1. Theoretical Bases for Educators of Adults

body of knowledge underpinning the adult education field are described in the Brunner, Dobbs, and Jensen citations at the end of the chapter.

Numerous topical areas could be discussed as adult education theory bases. The topics chosen for inclusion in this chapter as the bases for the next two major sections were obtained from analyzing the journal *Adult Education* and from reviewing several others of the cited sources. In the estimation of the writer, the categories represent those areas where considerable attention has been given by researchers and where considerable information is known.

Undoubtedly, many areas of research that should be addressed are not covered in this chapter. For examples, role theory, dogmatism, the use of community councils, motivational theory, ego stage development, recidivism, communications theory, compressed speech uses, reading and the cloze procedure,[1] non-traditional education, and community development are all topics that were addressed in at least one *Adult Education* article. However, space limitations and personal judgments by the author have limited the subjects to those about to be presented. In addition, interest areas like Adult Basic Education (the disadvantaged adult) and educational gerontology (the older adult) were also addressed in the journal. Both areas have a considerable body of knowledge already developed, much of which is reported in other sources or specifically focused journals (see the Bibliography).

BUILDING A THEORY BASE

The following subsections will contain summarizations of various research findings. In addition, where it appears plausible to do so, theoretical bases or

1. The cloze procedure is a method of systematically deleting words from a section of prose so that a reader's ability to accurately supply the deleted words can be measured.

evolving theory areas will be described. A brief analysis of what the research and theory mean for the adult educator will be found as the concluding remarks for each subsection. Certainly not all of the possible implications will be discussed. It is hoped that the reader and any interested researchers will utilize the information presented as a stimulation for future reflection, discussion, and theory development.

The Adult Education Participant

The adult education student has been studied often and in many ways. Adult education researchers and others began taking a concentrated look at adult participants in the 1930s and 1940s, trying to find out who they were and in what they were interested. The 1950s and 1960s were periods in which usable survey instruments and prediction scales for studying the adult education student were developed. The past few years have been a period where group and individual differences in participants have been examined.

One of the landmark examinations of adult participants was by Johnstone and Rivera in 1962 (see the Bibliography). Nearly 24,000 adults throughout the United States were interviewed to obtain information on their educational activities. Based on that information, it was estimated that approximately 25 million adults—more than one person in every five at that time—had been engaged in one or another form of educational endeavor. A great deal of that activity, nearly one-third, was in self-directed or independent study of some nature. About one-third of the endeavors were of a vocational nature and another one-fifth in the recreational sphere.

A 1972 survey (see Cross and Valley in the Bibliography) suggests that a significant increase in participation had taken place in the ten years between the two surveys. A usable sample of 1,893 respondents responded to questionnaires about their educational activity. From that information it was estimated that nearly one adult in every three is involved in some form of adult education. A greater involvement in recreational activity (approximately 42 percent), a slightly less involvement in vocational subjects, and a moderate increase in the study of general academic subjects were found when the 1972 information was compared with the 1962 data.

From the studies described above and from numerous additional research endeavors concentrating on fairly specific audiences, the following picture can be drawn of the participant in organized adult and continuing education. People who participate more than others in adult education are likely to be—

Younger.
Higher educated.
Members of more organizations.
Positive in their attitudes toward education and the educational agency.
Middle class.
Highly motivated to learn.

Urban residents with easy access to education.
Involved with broad and diverse leisure activities.
Highly skilled in social relationships.
Oriented in terms of a personal role of service to others.

People who participate less in adult education have been found to have lower incomes and socioeconomic levels, to maintain a fairly restricted social circle of friendships, to engage passively in sports, and to limit most of their activity to fairly immediate surroundings.

Specific audiences and users of specific types of adult education have also been studied by researchers. For example, the more highly educated, those with plans for further continuing education, and those individuals living in highly populated areas are more frequent users of the public library. As another example, it has been found that among adults with low educational achievement levels, the least educated, those under age 35 and over 65, unemployed individuals, homemakers, those with the fewest number of children, and people with the greatest withdrawal tendencies participated the least.

A number of reasons have been found as to why people participate in adult education. As described in Chapter 3, Houle theorizes that there are at least three basic reasons for participation in continuous educational activity: Some people had a specific goal in mind, some were activity or socially oriented, and some were just plain interested in constantly learning new things. Other reasons that have been determined include wanting to be a better informed person, to have initial or updating job information, to achieve a religious goal, to escape from environmental problems or pressures, and to comply with a formal requirement.

A variety of barriers to participation have also been uncovered. Some of the important reasons given as obstacles to participation are as follows:

Not wanting to go out in the evening.
Not enough time.
Financial limitations.
Home and job responsibilities.
Lack of energy or health problems.
Perception of being too old to learn.
Bureaucracy complexities.
Transportation limitations.
Child care problems.

What does information of this nature reveal about the field of adult education? The teacher, potential teacher, or program administrator should be able to derive several implications. For example, some of the barriers to participation can be lessened by offering formal adult education classes in neighborhood schools or community college buildings or even homes. Independent study opportunities, financial assistance, daytime courses, and reduced credit and other bureaucratic or formal requirements are also corrective possibilities.

In addition, knowledge that current participants tend to be highly education-oriented suggests that helping to promote a positive attitude toward education and learning among all citizens has the potential of prompting a greater utilization of education in the future.

Dropping Out and Perservering in Adult Education

Related closely to the accumulated information on participants in adult education is the research and evolving theory that exists as to why some people drop out of educational programs. No accurate national statistics are available on the percentage or number of dropouts in a given year, but it can range from none to a fairly high percentage in some classes or programs.

The research that has been completed on this topic enables the following picture to be drawn representing most dropouts. The dropout in comparison to the person who completes a course or program often has—

Less intelligence.
Lower reading abilities.
Experienced less success in past learning efforts.
Less education.
Lower vocabulary skills.
Had less success in work experiences.
Been out of school longer.
Had less experience in adult education.
To rely on public transportation to attend adult education activities.
Enrolled because of an educational or vocational deficiency.
A lower status job.
Lower income.
Been fairly inactive in community affairs.
Been less permanent in a community and at a residence.
Been more dissatisfied with the class and the teacher.

Note the many similarities between the picture drawn above and that describing the non-participant.

Several other findings are available. For example, younger people are more likely to drop out than older persons. Some researchers have suggested that age may be the most powerful factor in predicting who will drop out. Single individuals, females, minorities in an integrated learning environment, non-homeowners, and those having an inactive employment status who enroll in job-related education frequently drop out more than do their counterparts. If strictly credit adult education classes were examined, individuals with lower academic abilities tend to drop out more; however, people with higher academic abilities were more likely to drop out of noncredit classes. On the other hand, several research studies have shown no relationship between academic ability and a propensity to drop out when all forms of adult education are considered.

Some researchers have also looked at persons who finish adult education activities they start. They have found that perseverers are more likely to—

Perceive a persister as more worthy that a dropout.
Rate external and instrumental goals higher.
Have a definite goal as the reason for enrolling.
Be in smaller classes.
Have had a high school rank higher than dropouts.
Have received information about the education through mailed brochures.

Enrollment in hobby-related adult education, recency of past education, and personal motivation also have been found to be related to perseverance. One study reported, too, that professional and technical workers dropped out less than other occupational classifications.

Closely related to the idea of perseverance is the regularity of adult education class attendance. Researchers have found that the degree of course understanding, a person's fulfillment of needs, the approachability of the instructor, and the amount of formal and informal class interaction are related to attendance. In addition, research on class attendance occasionally has disclosed some rather surprising findings. In at least one study, attendance regularity and the sociability of one's classmates were found to be negatively related.

At lower socioeconomic and educational levels the dropout problem often is tied to vocational reasons. For example, dropouts from a manpower training program often had resided in areas with the greatest employment opportunities, had previous work experience in service occupations, had received higher incomes before training, had a history of unemployment, and had less education compared to those who did not drop out. Dropouts also reported less satisfaction with the training.

However, not all the reasons found for dropping out can be directly related to the student. For example, the stated requirements of the involved adult education agency, the reception given enrolling students, the informality of the learning setting, and the attention given to student needs—all have been found to be related to the dropout problem. Even the type of instructional method employed by the teacher and the course contents can have a bearing. More information on the instructional setting and teaching methods will be given in later subsections.

The adult educator should be able to derive various implications from the information presented above. Who are recruited into certain educational programs, supplemental and attention needs of potential dropouts, bureaucratic and administrative decision needs, and the classroom atmosphere requirements are all important elements of the learning environments. Perhaps the most important finding research of the nature described above reveals about adult education is that differences between persisters and dropouts do exist; consequently, continuous research will be required if a workable theory on helping all kinds of adults is to be developed.

Intelligence and Achievement Factors

The ability of the adult to achieve in educational settings has been studied by several researchers. In addition, adult intelligence has been of research interest for a number of years. For example Wechsler (see Bibliography) was a pioneer in researching adult intelligence. Although various IQ tests for adults exist with varying degrees of validity, the Wechsler Adult Intelligence Scale (WAIS) is one of the tests most often utilized for research and counseling purposes.

The achievement ability has been examined in many ways. One study showed that grades as a measure of achievement were related in a positive direction with advancing age, vocabulary levels, amount of education, and socioeconomic status. Other researchers have found that achievement is related in a positive direction to recency of education, to whether or not a person had participated previously in adult education, and to whether or not a person had formal college education. Another research effort found that the knowledge of humanities, social science, and history improved with age, whereas knowledge of mathematics and science decreased. Research on a specific type of adult student found that students in extension courses achieve as well as regular undergraduate students.

Related to achievement potential is the topic of attitudes. For example, considerable evidence is available to suggest a theory of increasing closed-mindedness with advancing age. One study found a negative relationship between achievement and overall social conformity (agreeing with others). However, a steadfast generalization cannot be drawn because such variables as the amount of education, religious affiliation, and income level can have a direct bearing on change potential. Indeed, some researchers have found no evidence of increased rigidity with age.

The implications of the above research and emerging theory are many. Obviously, adults have the potential to succeed with learning endeavors throughout their lives. Intelligence tests can be used with adults for a variety of reasons of interest to adult educators. In addition, prospective teachers of adults need to be cognizant of changes that take place with increasing age or decreasing income levels in order to make the appropriate adjustments within the classroom setting or in the development of learning materials.

Learning and Psychology

So much information, research data, and theory exist related to adult learning and psychology that it is impossible to do justice in describing the material in one small subsection. Adult educators, psychologists, and researchers from various disciplines have studied the adult learner for a number of years. Thus, only a summary of the information will be included here. The reader is referred to several of the sources described at the conclusion of this chapter for more detailed discussions.

Various researchers have isolated differences between adults and youth that can or do affect learning. For example, the following is known about learning and the aging process:

Speed of reaction and performance tend to decline with age.
Visual acuity frequently decreases over time.
Auditory acuity often decreases with advancing age.
Sensory acuity can become reduced in the later years.
Memory may become impaired over time, especially if poor initial learning existed.
Psychomotor skills tend to lessen with age increase.
Health declines can affect learning.

In addition, changes in attitudes, motivation, satisfaction, and self-concept are probable throughout the lifespan. Such changes and declines continuously affect a person's learning needs, interests, and abilities.

The findings on age differences are not intended to paint a gloomy picture for the older person in terms of learning. Quite the contrary, one of the most consistent findings about the adult as learner has centered around the potential to acquire new knowledge and skills throughout the entire lifespan. Early research on adult learning in the 1920s and 1930s showed gradual declines in learning potential with age. However, the removal of speed of performance in testing learning ability and various other factors have led most researchers to the conclusion that there is no apparent relationship between the age of a person and learning performance. Indeed, there is considerable evidence that older persons can learn some things better than younger persons because of their wealth of experience and, frequently, a more positive self-concept.

In addition, sex of the learner has not been found to be related to learning ability. However, recency of education, prior participation in adult education, health status, social status, and a variety of other factors are related to learning potential. The amount of education a person has also makes a difference, although the educationally disadvantaged can and do learn.

Thus, the educator responsible for facilitating learning by adults can expect individual differences, should take into account decreasing performance speeds, and should believe that every student has the potential for high achievement. In addition, various psychological and physiological factors, such as hearing and vision, change with increasing age; they have a relation to adult learning and instruction, which in turn can affect the selection of different teaching methods and materials. The next subsection discusses some of the research on methods and media usage in adult education.

Methods and Media

Considerable research on the use of various instructional methods and media with the adult learner has been completed. Perhaps the fact that experimental

research designs are fairly easy to establish by altering methods and media
has stimulated research in this area. Although continuing research is necessary,
some generalizations are possible and a theory of methods and media usage is
beginning to emerge.

One of the most frequently studied and compared method is the lecture—
the narrative transmittal of information to a class of students. The use of the
lecture with adult students is very widespread as would be expected, given the
educational traditions existing throughout the world and the administrative
necessity of classes and classrooms in most institutions. However, the lecture
does not have universal appeal nor has it been completely successful. The lecture
has been found to be best suited to the presentation of information for immediate recall uses; recall can be made even more effective when supplemental discussion or visual aids are used. Unfortunately, such information is often not
retained very long.

The intent here is not to be hypercritical of the lecture method. Lecturing
to students is often the only practical means for presenting certain information
and, indeed, some teachers will only feel comfortable with the lecture approach.
In addition, the lecture method and the appeal of the method to students will
be quite different from one situation to the next because of the content being
covered, the use made of supplemental learning aids such as visual materials,
and the amount of student-to-student or student-to-teacher interaction that is
possible. Consequently, the purpose of the next two paragraphs is to indicate
the effects of some variations.

For example, one study determined through follow-up testing that groups
of adults who obtained information by reading it did better than those who
were presented the material through lectures. Another study showed that
adult students had a significant preference for classes in which instructional
methods more novel than the lecture were used. Still another study found that
more than 70 percent of would-be adult learners preferred a method other
than lecture.

When the participants in lecture courses for credit were compared with
those in noncredit discussion groups the following differences were found:
Those in the lectures were younger, more often single, more educated, and
higher skilled occupationally. They also had less previous participation in
adult education. The opposite circumstances were found for those in the
discussion groups.

Placing people in groups in terms of compatibility, building group cohesive-
ness, and giving people group process skills are other methods or techniques
found to be successsful in promoting learning. Research has also found that
group learning activities and workshop settings were superior in promoting
learning when compared with learning that resulted from only reading
materials. Such a finding is probably not too surprising; however, short-term
workshops were found not effective in one study in altering long-term attitude

change. In another study it was found that the amount of in-class interaction was related to the regularity of attendance. Such research shows the complexities involved in attempting to build a theory on instructional methods or settings.

Various forms of media or specific instructional techniques have also been studied in relationship to the adult learner. Some reported findings are as follows:

Ability based on audiotape listening decreased with age.

Audiotape listening while reading the same material improved the comprehension of the material for undereducated adults.

Role playing is effective only if the group is adequately prepared for its use.

The use of nationally known personalities and the provision of some type of feedback mechanism improves the effectiveness of instructional television.

The reader should examine some of the sources at the end of the chapter for more information on the use of media and specific techniques for instruction.

It has also been found that various channels of communication or types of informational presentations, such as formal adult education courses, books, mass media forms, and demonstration each have clearly profiled audiences. For example, the lower the educational level the greater the desire for demonstration or case-study materials. Thus, knowledge obtained through experience and by reading about research like that described above should help the adult education teacher and administrator be more successful.

Program Planning and Administration

The operation of adult education programs or agencies is a task that requires broad and diverse skills. So has the research in this area been diverse. Planning adult education programs, evaluation, the assessment of needs, and administrative processes are some of the skills required and researched by adult educators.

Most of the research on needs analysis with adults is evolving toward a theory that suggests successful adult education programing is predicated on a determination and utilization of interests and wants that can be described in some way by prospective students. In other words, people participate in adult education because they want to become better informed, to be with people, or to be better prepared for a job; thus, the educational program needs to be directed toward such goals. However, there is evidence that determining what a person perceives as a need and what that same person demonstrates as a need may result in two entirely different findings, with the resulting programing efforts made more complicated.

There is also considerable research to support the notion that involving the adult student in the program-planning process is beneficial in terms of success. For example, in one study adults who participated in the establishment of course objectives were found to have more positive attitudes toward the learning experience after its completion than did those who had not helped to establish the objectives. Related research has shown that when students can examine the learning expectations ahead of the actual experiences in realistic, believable behavior, usually in terms of behavioral objectives, the learning is enhanced.

There is also some descriptive research available relative to what are the factors of a successful adult education program. Awareness of community needs, solid support for adult education by an educational board, local community help with the adult education activities, continuous evaluation, long-range planning efforts, flexibility in programing, good counseling services, and the use of many different materials as learning resources are some of the variables found to be important. Program planners and administrators should be able to utilize such findings in their own planning efforts.

Much of the remaining research in the area of program planning and administration has been scattered over a variety of topics:

The comparison of educational needs with economic needs.
When and where to charge fees for adult education courses.
Marketing and merchandising adult education opportunities.
The use of behavioral modification principles.
When and where to have adult education courses.

Many of the implications related to the research described above should be obvious in terms of planning and administering adult education programs. Teachers and administrators will also need to supplement the information with existing theory and research from education in general and from a broad range of behavioral science literature. In addition, more research on community-related problems, communication theory, interpersonal relationships, and the above topics will be required before a theoretical basis for adult education programing can be said to exist.

Teachers of Adults

The type of adult education teacher has received some research attention. For example, attendance regularity has been found to relate to the type of instructor, with a more approachable and interactive teacher more likely to experience higher attendance regularity from his or her students. More-experienced teachers were also found to misjudge more often than less-experienced teachers the importance attached by dropouts to an overall set of goals. However, Adult Basic Education teachers who had prior training in ABE were found in one study to have a higher retention rate among students.

Examinations of teaching styles have also been carried out. One study found that a permissive attitude in the classroom increased comprehension on the part of the adult student. Warm and expressive teachers received the most favorable evaluation in another study. The material in the next major section on a teaching and learning process known as *andragogy* will provide more discussion on styles of adult teaching.

There are several implications from such findings for the training of teachers. Most of the positive findings could also be used as bases for selecting teachers. However, more research on adult education teachers will be required before a generalizable body of knowledge can be made available.

EVOLVING THEORY AREAS

Andragogy

Andragogy (see the references by Knowles, 1970 and 1973a) is the name given a teaching and learning process designed for the adult learner and the adult education teacher. The process is predicated on beliefs that the adult-aged person is capable of self-direction, has unlimited learning potential, and possesses ever changing learning needs.

Five assumptions as bases for the process were evolved by Knowles:

1. A person at adulthood perceives himself or herself as capable of self-direction and self-motivation.
2. The experiences one brings to an educational setting are a rich resource for learning.
3. Learning should be related to the various developmental needs of an adult (spouse, parent, retired person, etc.).
4. A problem-centered orientation to learning is necessary for the adult student.
5. The adult learner wishes to immediately apply much of the new learnings acquired.

Translating such assumptions into a teaching/learning process implies that mutual needs-diagnosis and planning are necessary, the learner should be an important resource in the learning activity, and that the learning should be problem centered. Therefore, the teacher becomes a resource person, facilitates the process, and serves as an expert only when required to or when he or she has some special expertise.

Although a clearly defined theory of andragogy with an abundance of supporting research is not yet available, considerable support can be found in related research by others. Several researchers, for example, have found that student-centered education where the instructor serves as a facilitator of the learning by adults rather than a transmitter of knowledge is preferred and often the most effective. Evidence is also available that indicates if the participant is involved in planning a learning activity he or she will be more successful in that learning. In addition, there are research findings available that support the notion of learning being more effective if any related activities can make use of the participant's experience.

A great deal more research will be required to bring support and a fuller understanding of the above assumptions and procedural suggestions, most of which have been synthesized from related theory or based on teaching experience. However, the information available on andragogy provides an exciting area for future research and discussion.

The Adult's Learning Projects

Another exciting area of research is based on the initial work by Tough (see Chapter 3) and supplemented since then by several additional research efforts. Developing from this research is a theory pertaining to the self-directed adult learner and the potential adult educators have in facilitating such learning.

Following are some of the tentative conclusions that can be drawn from the research completed thus far:

1. Learning projects are carried out by almost every adult.
2. Learning in credit courses is only a small amount of the total learning carried out (usually less than 5 percent).
3. A majority of the learning is self-planned (approximately two-thirds).
4. Books, pamphlets, newspapers, friends, and relatives are the most important sources of information.
5. Most learning is practically oriented or of a self-fulfillment nature.
6. The home is the most preferred place of learning.

Traditionally, adult educators have dealt primarily with adult learning that takes place in organized classes or formal groups. However, the case made throughout this book with respect to the lifelong learning forces and the emerging changes required of adult educators make the research on adults' learning projects quite important. The implications center around how such learning can be facilitated, what roles can or should professional adult educators undertake, and what new skills will be required for educators. Obviously, more research is required before the total implications are understood or before a theory of working with the self-directed learner is understood. Hopefully, such research will be undertaken.

RESEARCH IN ADULT EDUCATION

A considerable amount of adult education research has already been completed as the discussion in the preceding chapters shows. Research even appears now to be a growing topic of interest and actual activity among professionals in the field. Certainly, continued research is needed if theoretical bases for adult and continuing education are to be established. Several sources cited at the end of the chapter will provide the interested reader or prospective researcher status or projective information relative to adult education research.

Not only is the research in adult education diverse and increasing in amount, it also appears that the kind of research being carried out is becoming more sophisticated. A great deal of research descriptive in nature is still being completed and is still needed; however, many adult education researchers are starting to ask "why?" questions in addition to "what?" and "where?" questions. Experimental designs, multiple variable manipulations and analyses, and annual adult education research seminars and conferences at the national and international levels are some of the changes taking place. In addition, the research skills of professionals coming from graduate departments of adult education are steadily improving. Such changes will not only affect the theory bases for the field, but will also have impact on policies and practice in adult education.

IMPLICATIONS FOR TEACHERS

Several implications have already been presented in the various sub-sections describing theoretical bases for adult education. Some of the research information presented is specific to the adult learner and some is generalizable to any age. Thus, it behooves the teacher of adults, experienced or new, to have as broad an understanding of the research and literature as possible because of the potential ramifications for curriculum design, in-class methodology, and person-to-person relationships with the student. Hopefully, the information presented and the sources cited at the end of the chapter will facilitate an initial understanding of the adult learner and of the adult education enterprise.

STUDY STIMULATORS

1. How does an understanding of a theory affect the approach a person takes in dealing with people?
2. Analyze your own teaching process in the light of the information presented in this chapter. Will your process need any changes to be effective with the adult learner?
3. Select ten adults at random. Determine the nature and amount of any adult education participation within the past year.
4. What differences would you believe exist between a person who is involved more often in organized adult education and one who is involved more often in self-directed learning?
5. Given what is known about people who are more likely to participate in formal adult education, how would your recruiting of people for adult education be affected?
6. Given what is known about people who are more likely to drop out of adult education programs, what would you attempt to do to reduce the incidence of dropping out?
7. Do you believe it is necessary or useful to know an adult's IQ? Examine and analyze one or more IQ tests used with adults.
8. What are the implications of the available data on adult achievement in terms of motivating adults to learn?

9. Describe some differences you perceive to exist between adults and youth in terms of learning needs and preferences.
10. Given some of the information known about the adult learner, how would you design a class for an audience of both adults and children?
11. What types of teaching methods would you employ with the adult learner? What use would you make of media and audiovisual aids?
12. How might you involve the adult student in planning and implementing an adult education course?
13. What are some implications for education from the theory and findings emerging from research on the adult's learning projects?
14. Suggest some future needs for the field of adult education in terms of research needs, questions to be answered, and theory-building requirements.

SELECTED BIBLIOGRAPHY

Books and Articles

"Adult Education," a special issue of *Review of Educational Research*, 29, No. 3 (June 1959). Research and literature related to learning, methods, administration, and other adult education topics are discussed by various authors.

BRUNNER, EDMUND DE S., et al. *An Overview of Adult Education Research*. Washington, D.C. (formerly Chicago): Adult Education Association of the USA, 1959. 279 pages. Index. In this excellent introduction to adult education research the authors examined theses and dissertations, *Adult Education* and other journals, books, monographs, and bulletins, and various other materials related to adult education. Chapters deal with learning, interests, participation, and methods, to name a few of the topics covered. Most chapters contain useful summaries and suggestions of additional research needs.

CROSS, K. PATRICIA, VALLEY, JOHN R., and Associates. *Planning Non-Traditional Programs*. San Francisco: Jossey-Bass, 1974. 263 pages. Subject and name indexes. Appendixes. Annotated bibliography. The book presents an overview of non-traditional study in the United States. A summary of a 1972 research project on adult participation in education, a survey of non-traditional opportunities, and technological uses in non-traditional programs are presented.

DICKINSON, GARY, and RUSNELL, DALE. "A Content Analysis of Adult Education," *Adult Education*, 21, No. 3 (Spring 1971), pp. 177–85. An analysis of the first 20 volumes of the journal *Adult Education* is presented.

DOBBS, RALPH C. (ed.). *Adult Education in America*. Cassville, Mo.: Litho Printers, 1970. 334 pages. The editor combines a series of reprinted and original articles over a broad range of topics. Research needs and various aspects of a theory base for adult education are discussed.

DUBIN, SAMUEL S., and OKUN, MORRIS. "Implications of Learning Theories for Adult Education," *Adult Education*, 24, No. 1 (Fall 1973), pp. 3–19. This article presents a review of the major learning theories and discusses their relevance for adult learning.

HIEMSTRA, ROGER. *The Older Adult and Learning*. Lincoln, Nebr.: Department of Adult and Continuing Education, University of Nebraska, Lincoln, 1975 (also in the ERIC system). 106 pages. Appendixes. This publication reports on research carried out in Nebraska with adults 55 years of age and older. Obstacles preventing participation in adult education, learning preferences, and actual learning activities are described.

JOHNSTONE, JOHN W. C., and RIVERA, RAMON J. *Volunteers for Learning*. Chicago: Aldine Publishing Co., 1965. 624 pages. Index. Appendixes. This massive volume reports on the educational activities of nearly 24,000 adults living in the United States. Educational opportunities for adults are included. A variety of tables support the narration.

KNOWLES, MALCOLM S. *The Adult Learner: A Neglected Species*. Houston: Gulf Publishing Co., 1973a. 198 pages. Author and subject indexes. Appendixes. Bibliography. In this book Knowles describes and compares various theories. He relates much of the discussion and various research findings to the andragogical teaching and learning process. The six appendixes provide useful supplemental information on learning and the adult potential.

———. "Sequential Research Needs in Evolving Disciplines of Social Practice," *Adult Education*, 23, No. 4 (Summer 1973b), pp. 298–303. The author suggests the various kinds of research needed as a field of study develops.

———. "What Do We Know About the Field of Adult Education," *Adult Education*, 14, No. 2 (Winter 1964), pp. 67–79. A description of the field, its professional associations, and its operation in the early 1960s.

KNOX, ALAN B. "The ERIC Clearinghouse Serves the Field of Adult Education During a Year of Transition," *Adult Education*, 25, No. 3 (Spring 1975), pp. 192–97. A description of the services and resources available to adult educators through the ERIC Clearinghouse.

KREITLOW, BURTON W. *Educating the Adult Educator: Part 2. Taxonomy of Needed Research*. Theoretical Paper No. 13, Report from the Adult Re-Education Project. Madison, Wisc.: Center for Cognitive Learning, University of Wisconsin, 1968. 20 pages. This report contains a concise analysis of needed research in adult education. Research questions are presented throughout the discussion on the adult learner, the adult in society, and the adult education enterprise.

———. "Federal Support to Adult Education: Boon or Boondoggle?" *Adult Education*, 25, No. 4 (Summer 1975), pp. 231–37. A discussion is included of needed research in adult education with an analysis of how federal support has affected the nature and amount of research.

LONG, HUEY B., and AGYEKUM, STEPHEN K. "*Adult Education* 1964–1973: Reflections of a Changing Discipline," *Adult Education*, 24, No. 2 (Winter 1974), pp. 99–120. An analysis of the articles appearing in the journal *Adult Education* over a nine-year period. The articles were described in terms of the kind, content, and discovered trends.

LONG, HUEY B., and HIEMSTRA, ROGER (eds.). *Graduate Research in Adult Education*. In press. To be published as *Part I, Handbook Series in Adult Education*, 1976. Various authors contributed chapters on research needs, research trends, and types of research used in adult education. The publication is designed as a companion piece for other publications on research design and theory.

MANJO, ANTHONY V; LORTON, MARY; and CONDON, MARK W. F. *Personality Characteristics and Learning Style Preferences of Adult Basic Education Students*. Research Monograph. Kansas City, Mo.: Center for Resource Development in

Adult Education, School of Education, University of Missouri–Kansas City, 1975.
49 pages. Appendix. References. The researchers utilized three instruments to
identify personality characteristics and learning styles of ABE students. ABE
students tended to be more aggressive, intense, and conflict-prone in comparison
with other undereducated adults and they preferred to learn by more direct
teaching approaches as opposed to less direct approaches.

MATARAZZO, JOSEPH D. *Wechsler's Measurement and Appraisal of Adult Intelligence.*
Baltimore: Williams & Wilkins, 1972. 572 pages. Index. Author index. Bibliography. Appendixes. The author describes the nature and assessment of intelligence and discusses validating intelligence tests. He also describes the earlier
Bellevue test and the later Wechsler Adult Intelligence Scales (WAIS). This publication presents updated information to the Wechsler source cited below.

MEZIROW, JACK. "Toward a Theory of Practice," *Adult Education,* 21, No. 3
(Spring 1971), pp. 135–47. This article suggests a rationale and strategy for developing an adult education theory base. The grounded theory research procedure is
described and suggested as a research tool with great potential.

SPEAR, GEORGE E. (Project Director). *Adult Basic Education National Teacher
Training Study, Part 1: Review of Literature.* Kansas City, Mo.: University of
Missouri, 1972. 137 pages. An annotated review of literature related to Adult
Basic Education, the undereducated adult, and general adult education. More than
400 citations are included.

WECHSLER, DAVID. *The Measurement of Adult Intelligence.* Baltimore: Williams &
Wilkins, 1944. 258 pages. Index. Appendixes. Intelligence quotients tables.
Manual of introduction and the tests. This early classic describes the nature and
classification of adult intelligence with a description of the developmental process
involved in constructing an adult intelligence test.

Additional references cited in other chapters:

Chapter 3. Houle	Chapter 4. Jensen, et al.
Okes	Knowles
Tough	

Periodicals

Adult Education (USA), *Adult Education* (Great Britain), *Adult Leadership, Australian
Journal of Adult Education, Convergence, Dissertation Abstracts* (International),
Educational Gerontology, Indian Journal of Adult Education, Journal of Extension,
and the *TESOL Quarterly* are some recommended periodicals containing research
and theory information relevant to the field of adult education.

CHAPTER 8

Trends and Projections

People have probably always been interested in the future—in wanting to understand it, control it, predict it, and even invent it. However, projecting into the future can be risky, scary, and perhaps even impossible. The purpose of this chapter will be to extrapolate from much of the information presented in the previous chapters some trends apparent in society and, more specifically, several trends of an educational nature. Such information should be useful in helping the interested reader think and plan ahead for his or her own personal and professional involvement in life.

FUTURE PROJECTING

Those individuals who spend a good deal of their time predicting or projecting into the future usually use one of two methods. One method is to examine the present, determine some trends, and project those trends into the future in conjunction with various expectations related to population change, environmental factors, and analyses of human behavior. The second method is to simulate a future date in time, carry out some future-inventing activities, and then determine what type of activities or changes would be necessary to achieve the future that was invented.

There are strengths and weaknesses to either method. Projecting from trends is usually a very logical activity and a certain amount of reliability is built into the process. However, slight changes in behavior at the individual or societal level can alter trends significantly in only a few years. Inventing the future and finding ways to get there usually is an exciting process. Problems arise when all the many changes required to alter an existing trend or to start some new trend are attempted. Indeed, some individuals contend that the future cannot be invented and that we must learn to live with changes as they occur.

Responding to change and creating change are both possible in the estimation of the author. The Toffler impact related to the future shock theme in many ways painted a rather gloomy and pessimistic view of the future. However, just knowing about the possibilities of an undesirable future could be the very impetus needed to cause those changes in people necessary for adjusting to rapid social change. It is suggested that what is needed is a constant study of the future as a means of having the best information for planning.

Predicting the future of adult and continuing education has been attempted fairly rigorously in the past few years. For example, the Educational Policy

99

Research Center at Syracuse University has initiated a project entitled the Future of Adult Education and Learning. The strategy the center utilizes combines an analysis of trends through various data-gathering efforts with a futures invention methodology that involves the participation of people most likely to be affected by the plans and decisions of experts and policymakers. The information resulting from the process is both disseminated widely and utilized in the analysis and formation of policy.

Adult educators from throughout the United States in the past four years have been participating in a similar process stimulated from an initial grant by the U.S. Office of Education for a national adult education think tank on the future. Workshops held throughout the country have enabled adult educators and adult education participants to develop plans for the future. There is some evidence that the project's impact is beginning to be felt through changing policy at the national level.

SOCIETAL TRENDS

Before the future can be invented or even before some projections regarding the future can be made, it is important to understand ourselves, the society in which we exist, and the environment that surrounds us. Subsequently, this section will outline two major trends affecting American society, suggest some implications for education, and summarize several other trends.

The Increase of Leisure

There are many societal indications that time for leisure in the United States is increasing. Longer vacation periods, shorter work weeks, early retirements, and longer lives are some of the indicators. Such a trend, if in fact actually taking place, will have long-ranging implications for the field of adult education in the form of increasing time for learning.

However, there are several reasons why the apparent increase in time for leisure may not be as great as what appears at first glance. For example, the general affluence of many people in the United States permits the pursuit of recreational activity to a degree that would have been economically impossible only a few years ago. In addition, many other people have found that inflation, various forms of injustice, and the pressures of living in a time of rapid social change have forced their utilization of leisure time to take on an extra job, to save money somehow in the home environment (e.g., a family garden), to carry out some necessary community service, or to simply come to better grips with their own lives.

Nor do we understand very well what happens to people when they use their leisure in various ways. The person who spends three weeks out of the year hurrying in the family camper to visit more places than last year may be contributing to the very pressures that cause the need for the vacation. The person who spends hundreds of hours each year glued to a television set watching athletes bump, crash, and grind across the screen or watching hundreds of violent deaths in all sorts of ways may be developing into a valueless individual who expects that much of life is something owed to him or her by others. Not enough is known about the so-called leisure society and considerably more study will be required before all the ramifications can be determined.

The Changing Family Setting

Although the changing family setting was discussed in considerable detail in Chapter 2, some of the significant changes need to be accented here. For example, family units are becoming smaller. Fewer children, childless marriages, and single parent families are common throughout the United States. In addition, divorces, separations, remarriages and multiple family experiments seem to be continuously on the increase. New roles are also being assumed by family members.

The implications from various of these changes have been or will be experienced by most of us. What long-range effects such changes will have on society are not known nor can they be easily predicted. Some authorities even wonder if the family as a basic institutional setting in which most people begin their lives will survive much longer. This area, too, is in need of constant study and the various changes that do evolve will affect tomorrow's educator in many ways.

Additional Trends

There are many additional trends that perhaps deserve special attention. The continual increase in technology, a growing awareness of resource limitations or shortages, the growing gap between the rich and the poor, the constancy of new knowledge, the growth toward a service-oriented society, a continual march toward Orwell's 1984, the increasing mobility of people, the increase of crime throughout the country, and the growth of mental illness–related problems are only a few of those that can be mentioned. The interested reader can utilize several of the sources cited at the end of the chapter for further study. Each trend that one can verbalize will no doubt have numerous implications for education.

ARE WE AT A CROSSROAD?

There are some indications that the society existing as the United States, and even the world society, is at a crossroad in the evolution of mankind. Such a suggestion is, of course, easy to make but difficult to verify. Indeed, writers have been predicting either the end of the world or the development of a utopia for many, many years. However, the purpose of this section is to show that for whatever the reasons, many of which have been suggested in the preceding discussion, our society may be at a turning point from which humans will either emerge as better beings, more free and achieving at a higher potential than what is now possible, or as primarily repressed groups of mininations living under conditions of near poverty and illiteracy.

The beginning indications of this turning point stemmed mainly from the emergence of third-world countries and leaders. Smaller nations have been demanding attention and a greater share of the world's wealth, most noticeably in the past one or two decades. Indeed, solid demonstrations of the potential economic power of quite small countries have been witnessed by most people in the world through the existing crises related to fuel shortages. Individuals like Ivan Illich, Paulo Freire (see Bibliography), and Martin Luther King have also been able to command worldwide attention in connection with the plights of poor and oppressed people.

In the United States there are several indications of significant changes taking place in society. People are living alternative lifestyles and others have stopped shunning those that do. The aftermath of the Watergate scandal has been new laws affecting politicians, and there is evidence that new types of people are being attracted to positions of political leadership—people who are independent, tough, honest, and open.

Perhaps the most significant event has been the rapid growth of, and increasing attention to, the human potentiality movement. Interest in relaxation techniques, participation in human growth activities, and attempts by many to become more self-sufficient within the constraints of environmental limitations are all activities that have indicated people are interested in controlling and improving the quality of their own lives.

The implications of such changes are many and almost too hopeful in nature to be believable by a society of people who have experienced wars, economic depressions, and a variety of social unrest activities. However, an eternally optimistic person can once again see hope for where society is heading because free men and women, people who are capable of continued self-growth, and people who can be open and honest with one another should do as much, and, hopefully, more than anyone else to date in combating intolerance, in improving literacy, and in making the best decisions regarding economic and political matters. If such individuals do become the leaders of tomorrow and if such a movement can be extended throughout the world, a new type of society will emerge that may well be utopian in nature.

TRENDS AND ISSUES IN HIGHER EDUCATION

At times it is impossible to distinguish between the various levels of education. Where higher education leaves off and adult education begins is frequently difficult to determine. Trying to describe lifelong learning possibilities without referring to all levels of education or all age groupings of people is also difficult. In addition, education at the K–12 level is connected to college education or adult education by the learning skill levels and attitudes formed in youth. However, the intent of this section is to delineate some trends and issues affecting colleges and universities that have potential linkages to adult and continuing education.

For example, the potential of the community college in facilitating learning for adults is largely untapped. Adult education activities through the community service arms of community colleges have been on the increase during the past decade; however, there is considerable evidence that much more growth is possible, especially through such services as educational opportunities away from the campus setting, through learning resource centers, and through a variety of non-traditional class settings. In addition, the community college is perhaps the best candidate at the community level to bring about some coordination to the many educational activities available and possible for adults.

Another issue of concern to most higher education administrators is the financial support available for programing. Federal and private sources are becoming more difficult to obtain, tax dollar support is being scrutinized much more carefully, and the ability of students to further increase the amount they pay for higher education is limited. Such problems will in many ways force institutions of higher education to become more efficient and more careful in their long-range planning. However, the issue of maintaining quality is a plaguing concern. One implication is that some colleges and universities will attempt to "cash in" on the adult education market as a means of new support.

An important trend primarily observed in the 1970s has been the rapid interest in and growth of non-traditional education. Implying primarily the provision of alternative learning opportunities through a variety of modes, non-traditional education programs are now available in almost every state of the Union. Some examples include the Empire State College (New York), the Minnesota Metropolitan State College, and the State University of Nebraska. Employing such non-traditional modes as performance contracting, internships, credit for experience, learning resource centers, and television classes, such institutions offer college degrees for people who will experience few or no traditional college classes.

As a result of the non-traditional movement, credentialism and its relationship to the traditional college or technical school preparation programs is receiving more attention. This has resulted in an increased examination of the competencies needed for certain occupations, the use of non-credit learning experiences, the alternatives to the granting of letter grades as an evaluation means, and ways to improve the technology and delivery systems for education. Although such activities will not change the approach to education overnight, they are encouraging signs that higher education is responding to some of the lifelong learning forces described in the first chapter.

TRENDS SPECIFIC TO ADULT AND CONTINUING EDUCATION

The first chapter, specifically, and portions of several other chapters alluded to several forces or needs that have helped to stimulate the lifelong learning movement and the increased interest in adult education. Rapid social change, high numbers of individuals with little or no education, the need for constant retraining, the variety of special audiences to be reached, and the discovery of the active self-directed learner are some of these forces and needs.

Other forces described above, such as an apparent increasing leisure, the influence of the third world, the predictions of futurists, and the potential of alternative or greatly different lifestyles, will also have impact on the field of adult education and the lifelong learning movement in many ways. Consequently, the purpose of this section is to describe apparent trends specific to adult and continuing education as a prelude to describing a variety of needs remaining to be met.

Increasing Participation

The tremendous increase in the number of adults participating in various forms of adult and continuing education has already been supported in earlier chapters. There is every reason to believe that such increases will continue, especially considering the many forces described above. Continuing professional education needs, for example, should continue to rapidly expand. In addition, the discovery of the immense activity by self-directed learners through the Tough research model (see Chapters 3 and 7) has added an entirely new dimension to analyzing participation trends.

The implications are many. The most obvious one is the vast opportunity for educators to find ways to meet such needs. Large numbers of newly trained adult educators will be required and many educators who now work mainly with children or college-age students must also become more skilled in facilitating the education of adults. More and better programs, new instructional techniques, many additional resources for learning, and new approaches to reaching people will also be required.

Marginality Versus Acceptance

The various forces already discussed and the rapid growth in participation are helping most adult educators move from a status of marginality in institutional or community settings to one of being accepted, understood, and even supported. That is not to say that adult educators are yet equal partners with other educators, nor are financial support dollars increasing very rapidly. However, the general field of education is very aware of the growth in adult education and in many institutions a more "equal billing" is being given to adult education programs.

The implications here, too, are numerous. Increased recognition will not only facilitate the increase and improvement of adult education programs, but will also help adult education professionals increase their impact on people because of the legitimizing spillover. Being able to meet with other educators on an equal footing should provide opportunities for significant interchanges which affect research, instructional methodologies, and the interrelationships possible between education at all levels. Indeed, the biggest benefit for adult educators to be derived from the move away from marginality is a better understanding of the entire lifelong learning concept.

Financial Support for Adult Education

The trend with regard to financial support for adult education at national, state, community, and private source levels has been a general increase in monies available during the past decade. A renewed interest by certain foundations in adult education, increases in the area of Adult Basic Education, efforts to federally finance lifelong learning through some type of voucher system (see Chapter 1), and new sources at the community and national levels because of community education interests have been mainly responsible for the increases. In addition, there are indications that proprietary institutions will support increasing amounts of adult education. The Rand Corporation, for example, now offers masters and doctoral degrees in the management area. The economic problems of the mid-seventies have slowed the increase in some cases and increased the need for a tighter accountability, but the various lifelong learning forces should continue to stimulate increased support and involvement.

There are implications related to this increasing support and the related tighter controls on how those monies are spent. Most adult education administrators have, out of necessity, become better at assessing needs, setting realistic goals, and evaluating the effectiveness of various programing efforts. In some cases tough decisions have had to be made to phase out or make smaller some adult education programs because of newly emerged needs. There have also been efforts in many communities and states to do a better job of coordinating adult education activities. Finally, many collegiate departments of adult education have merged with other units in order to become more efficient. All of these activities should benefit the adult education field over time.

Lifelong Learning Versus Lifelong Education

The lifelong learning movement has stimulated considerable attention in adult education and its potential for affecting people throughout their lives. Indeed, many adult educators have suggested that a new philosophy about learning is developing in people, a philosophy that allows adult education activities to be seen as a way of life rather than as remedial activities.

However, lifelong learning is becoming a status quo concept as interpreted by some people rather than a means for continuous learning. In other words, many individuals and groups have interpreted this movement as meaning education must be made lifelong rather than learning being an individual choice. For example, many professionals must take a certain number of courses or participate in preselected learning activities because of relicensure or certification requirements. In addition, the Continuing Education Unit (see Chapter 1) has been interpreted in several cases as a means for granting credit or recognition to almost any type of educational activity rather than as a means for identifying quality learning experiences outside of the more traditional credit mode. Both examples have tended to protect credentialism as a means for segmenting people or occupational classifications.

One implication is that the excitement of discovering learning as a new way of life or as a means of freeing the mind to permit continuous personal growth may be subjugated to a variety of institutional or profit-oriented constraints. Perhaps the adult education field is also at a crossroads, with one direction being lifelong learning as a means for creating a radically new way of life and the other direction being lifelong education as a highly structured and required means for developing people in an occupational, psychological, or sociological sense.

Technological and Instructional Advances

New technologies and instructional methodologies are continuously being developed. For example, new uses for the computer related to instruction and record keeping are evolving. Television and radio as tools in facilitating learning are in a stage of rapid development. Various audiovisual support systems, individualized learning processes, and concepts like the learning resource center are also being experimented with in conjunction with adult learning.

Increasing attention is also being given to the approaches appropriate in facilitating learning for the adult, many of which have been described in earlier chapters. The deemphasis on grading, involving the learner more in determining the content, decreasing the formality or traditionalism in the class setting, and experimenting with alternative approaches to the classroom setting as a basis for learning are some of the changes taking place.

Certainly such advances will continuously affect the adult education field. New people may be reached and instructional skills may improve. However, the financial support needs will increase in many instances and the problems of training or retraining adult educators to use the new advances will be many. A careful evaluation of the advances or changes must be made.

The Self-Directed Learner

The discovery of the vast amount of learning by adults that takes place each year outside of formal classrooms has been mentioned several times. However, the significance of such a discovery is not yet really understood. As research procedures become refined there are many indications that the high level of involvement will be found to be fairly consistent irrespective of such variables as location, amount of education, age, economic status, and occupational history. Consequently, adult learning opportunities will increasingly be of a self-directed nature.

The implications for the adult and continuing educator are related to both the right and the responsibilities involved with seeking to serve the self-directed learner. "Should such learning be assisted and, if so, to what degree?" are philosophical questions that must be answered. In addition, learning how to create better educational resources, how to help learners become more efficient, and how to help activate the many potential learning resources available at the community level and in a variety of non-education institutions are all activities that require immediate attention.

The Human Services Area

Much of the training effort related to adult education until recently has been concentrated in such areas as literacy training, manpower development, and the preparation of administrators, teachers, and researchers in adult education. However, there is considerable evidence that the training emphasis in adult education is moving more toward the human services area. For instance, nurses, social workers, law enforcement officials, county health workers, religious workers, and a variety of other people who must deal with adults and human behavior are increasingly looking to adult education for their in-service training and even for their graduate training. As another example, the development of learning resource centers in many communities is providing a new type of service to adults. Such human service opportunities should be even greater in the near future.

Where such a trend will take the field of adult and continuing education is not easily discernible. Certainly American society is becoming more service oriented and the time is near when the majority of occupational positions will be related to providing some sort of human service. Graduate adult education programs will need to change, experienced adult education professionals will need to adapt, and much greater bases of knowledge regarding the adult and human behavior will be required.

Additional Areas

There are several additional areas that must be at least mentioned. Systematic planning and the use of such planning tools as management by objectives or the development of comprehensive evaluation plans should increase. The interest in competencies, coping skills, and adult performance levels will most likely affect the approaches used in literacy training—preventive skills in the way of knowing how to learn rather than remedial skills may well be the philosophy that emerges. Carrying out a better coordination of the many educational activities and opportunities in a community is a real possibility within the next few years. A variety of new roles for teachers as mentors, learning resource center directors, and counselors are evolving. There are also indications that a new era of international cooperation with regard to adult education is beginning to take place. There are undoubtedly many additional trends that should have been mentioned or that will emerge in the very near future.

SEVERAL AREAS OF NEED

There are many areas important to the lifelong learning movement that require attention in the way of research, increased support, or decision making. Many of these needs have been discussed or alluded to in earlier chapters. However, the purpose of this section will be to highlight several of the areas of need in the hope that interested educators and leaders in the adult education field will have some bases for focusing much of their future attention.

The Training Need of Adult Educators

Most of the trends described in the above sections have direct ramifications for the training of adult educators at undergraduate, graduate, and in-service levels. In addition to the increasing emphasis on understanding human behavior that was alluded to, adult educators will certainly need to know increasingly more about the learning process and how effective learning is facilitated. Such educators, if they are to translate this knowledge into educational programs and services, will also need to become highly skilled in needs-diagnosis, in program planning, in utilizing new technology, and in facilitating learning for a variety of non-traditional formats.

Future adult educators will also need to be thoroughly grounded in community theory and the various strategies available for working with a variety of community groups and institutions. A related need is understanding the broad field of adult education and its historical importance in relation to individuals, communities, and society. In some instances a person may need to become thoroughly familiar with the operation of a specific agency or clientele group, but such specificity should not be at the expense of a broad understanding of the role and programs important to all of adult education.

Another important need is the ability to maintain a thorough understanding of contemporary society as it evolves, changes, and creates entire new sets of educational opportunities. Such a suggestion calls for educators to become future oriented, to constantly analyze trends and projections, and to frequently question their own roles in society.

Learner-Oriented Needs

There are several groups of learners or potential learners who have special needs that could be better served. Chapter 1 has a listing of various audiences with special needs. Handicapped adults, minority individuals, individuals in institutions, older adults, and women are some of those with crucial needs. Adult educators will be required to discover and utilize new approaches to working with such people.

The case already made concerning the self-directed learner suggests several related needs. Making more and better resources available for learning are important starts that must be made. In addition, several more difficult challenges requiring attention are helping people improve their self-learning abilities, helping learners judge their own competencies and actual needs, and helping learners become better planners in order to match available resources with discovered needs.

Another important need is for better instructional models. In other words, much more about the uniqueness of the adult learner and about adult-oriented instructional techniques must be known. This implies that more research and verification of the andragogical assumptions and many other aspects of adult education are needed. In addition, a better understanding of how to work with the learner in non-traditional settings is vitally needed.

Community-Level Needs

Considerable attention has already been given in this and in other chapters to the close relationship between adult educators and activities within the community setting. One of the related needs involves identifying the many resources potentially available for education and finding ways to activate their usage by learners.

Another closely allied need is learning how to provide a better coordination of educational programs and opportunities for adults. This will entail an enhanced communication to citizens of a community regarding available resources, the plugging in of the best resources to meet a certain need, and the facilitation of adult educators representing various agencies or institutions working in closer and supportive harmony. Whether such a need can be met through ad hoc relationships or whether one agency should perform such a role is still to be determined. However, the linking together of a community, its needs, and its resources is a logical requirement for surviving in a complex tomorrow.

Needs at the Leadership Level

There are several needs visible at the leadership level that are fairly difficult to articulate and probably just as difficult to correct. For example, most adult educators have a much greater potential for power within society than is assumed. The very nature of the type of person who gravitates to positions of service and who receives gratifications from seeing others grow and change instead of from constant product accomplishments often precludes his or her undertaking an active lobbying or even political role. However, it is contended that future adult educators must fill a much larger role in establishing public policies, especially those that have an impact on learning needs.

Another need is for adult educators to begin removing their institutional blinders. Most educators are tied so tightly to a variety of rules, regulations, and approaches to teaching that innovations are next to impossible. In addition, many adult educators confine themselves to only one small part of the educational field. Keeping in touch with other professionals, understanding change that takes place in other disciplines, and viewing lifelong learning as a movement that is affecting all age groups are important needs.

Expanding the extension of college offerings to off-campus sites, learning to utilize the various emerging non-traditional approaches, and working to keep such non-traditional approaches from becoming institutionalized or used only from a profit-oriented motive are also important needs. It is the contention of the author that adult educators have a potential to be the main leaders in the lifelong learning movement and in developing the various alternatives necessary for the non-traditional approach to learning. However, it will take knowledgeable professionals who are willing to change, to grow, and, themselves, to continuously learn, if such leadership needs are to be met.

OPPORTUNITIES FOR EDUCATORS

The many factors that have contributed to the lifelong learning movement and the continuous growth of adult education programs and activities have created many opportunities for educators as teachers, counselors, and administrators. There are many jobs open on a part-time basis, for example, and increasingly on a full-time basis, for teachers trained primarily to work with K–12 audiences. Retraining through in-service training or graduate degrees is often necessary to obtain or hold such positions or simply because many teachers suddenly find themselves working with adults. Thus, future K–12 teachers in their initial training should consider adding course work in, and exposure to, adult and continuing education.

The opportunities are wide ranging. At the community-wide level the educator as a resource person can work with a variety of non-school organizations helping with various planning, evaluating, and instructional needs. Increasingly agencies or businesses must respond to the rapid explosion of knowledge or the advent of new technology, and they frequently require help in designing in-service training sessions for employees, developing instructional materials, and evaluating learning activities. Therefore, it is suggested that educators make themselves more available as community resources.

Part-time teachers are constantly needed in the area of adult and continuing education. For example, many K–12 teachers across the country have been able to gain new skills through in-service training or, through experience, have adapted their previous skills and are employed in Adult Basic Education, adult high school, or GED (high school equivalency diploma) programs. Community and junior colleges, too, have an increasing need for teachers skilled or willing to become skilled in working with adults as teachers or curriculum specialists. Many of the special audiences described in Chapter 1 are also being reached through a variety of educational efforts which require teaching and other kinds of programing assistance.

The interest in non-traditional delivery systems and in the self-directed adult learner is also beginning to create new opportunities. Learning resource centers are being created in many communities, requiring educators with a variety of skills. The entire community education movement just now receiving federal attention and support has and will continue to create a need for increased educational assistance at the local school level. Undoubtedly many of these pressures will create positions and opportunities not even dreamed of yet, but the dynamic nature of adult education is what makes it such an interesting field with which to be associated.

STUDY STIMULATORS

1. The "future shock" theme suggests that many people are already reacting to the problems of change being too rapid through increasing suicide rates, mental breakdowns, and social disorders. If these events are related to rapid change what are some of the implications for educators?
2. Select a trend in education, such as increasing dropout rates, declining national achievement test scores, or something else you are aware of, and project it into the twenty-first century. What are the implications for education both now and in the future?
3. Simulate the year 2000 and pick out one or two things in education or in adult education that you would like to see take place by then. What is required in the way of policy, decision making, and programs to get there?
4. Select any one of the societal trends described in the first part of the chapter and derive some implications for both K–12 and adult educators.
5. Identify any non-traditional education opportunities in or nearest to your community.
6. What are the implications of the non-traditional movement for high schools and the educational preparation of youngsters?
7. Select any one of the trends suggested as specific to adult education and determine how your life as an educator or as a person interested in education will be affected.
8. Given the information presented in this book, what type of skills would you suggest an adult educator should have to be effective?

SELECTED BIBLIOGRAPHY

BLAKELY, EDWARD J., et al. "Prospects for a Learning Society," *Adult Leadership* 24, No. 1 (September 1975), pp. 34–45. Several authors contribute articles to this special section on the learning society. The problems of, and roles for, adult educators are discussed.

BLAZE, WAYNE, et al. *Guide to Alternative Colleges and Universities*. Boston: Beacon Press, 1974. 141 pages. Alphabetical and geographic indexes. Curricular index. The authors have brought together a wealth of information pertaining to alternative education opportunities. Special programs, free universities, and external degree programs are described.

BORGSTROM, GEORG. *The Food & People Dilemma*. North Scituate, Mass.: Duxbury Press, A Division of Wadsworth Publishing Company, Belmont, Calif., 1973. 140 pages. Index. Selected references. Appendix. The author explores the interactions of agriculture with food and resource consumption. He argues that the food-and-people issue is of such paramount significance to man's future that we must rapidly remedy the many related problems and make drastic revisions in our use of food.

CASE, CHARLES W., and OLSON, PAUL A. (eds.). *The Future: Create or Inherit*. Lincoln, Nebr.: Dean's Committee, Study Commission on Undergraduate Education, and the Education of Teachers, University of Nebraska—Lincoln, 1974. 238 pages. The book presents a discussion of the significance of future priorities for educators and describes some specific research and development priorities. Another valuable aspect of the book is a dialog section with educators and futurists on future planning methodologies and how to involve the community in future planning.

DIDSBURY, HOWARD F., JR. "Studying the Future: A Social Imperative," *Adult Leadership*, 22, No. 10 (April 1974), p. 318. A discussion of why adult educators should study the future.

DRUCKER, PETER F. *The Age of Discontinuity*. New York: Harper & Row, 1968. 394 pages. Index. The author describes the implications of technology on knowledge and talks about a world economy. The problems in society and the constant need for new knowledge are also discussed.

FAURE, EDGAR, et al. *Learning to Be*. Paris: UNESCO, 1972. 313 pages. Index. Appendixes. The book begins with a description of the history and current status of education. The authors then turn to the future needs of education in relationship to society. Some future needs, technological trends, and goals are described and a case made for a learning society.

FREIRE, PAULO. *Cultural Action for Freedom*. Cambridge, Mass.: Center for the Study of Development and Social Change, 1970. 55 pages. Appendix. A long-time advocate of human rights, the author talks about the adult literacy process and the raising of consciousness through what he calls "conscientization."

————. *Pedagogy of the Oppressed*. New York: Herder & Herder, 1970. 186 pages. Index. The author talks about a pedagogy that must be developed with and not for the oppressed people. Utilizing education in the struggle for liberation is the basic theme.

FULLER, R. BUCKMINSTER. *Utopia or Oblivion*. New York:Bantam Books, 1969. 366 pages. Bibliography. The author talks about the prospects for humanity in the future in the light of technology, decreasing resources, and international conflicts. His thesis is that utopia is possible and our only hope. The chapter on design strategy contains a tremendous amount of information and some ideas all educators should consider.

GILLETT, MARGARET. *Educational Technology: Toward Demystification*. Ontario: Prentice-Hall of Canada, 1973. 144 pages. Index. Appendixes. The intent of the author is to foster an understanding of educational technology from a humanistic viewpoint. She discusses and describes the use of various media and the computer.

GRABOWSKI, STANLEY M. (ed.). *Paulo Freire: A Revolutionary Dilemma for the Adult Educator.* Syracuse, N.Y.: Publications in Continuing Education, Syracuse University, 1972. 136 pages. Annotated bibliography. Several authors discuss the implications of Freire's work and philosophy for the adult educator. The bibliography is an excellent resource guide.

HOULE, CYRIL O. *The Design of Education.* San Francisco: Jossey-Bass, 1972. 323 pages. Index. Glossary. Bibliographic essay. In this unique volume Houle presents a case for the development of a program design process necessary for education. Interesting examples and a useful philosophy for education are displayed throughout the book. The bibliographic essay should be a special bonus for most educators.

HUSEN, TORSTEN. *The Learning Society.* London: Methuen, 1974. 268 pages. Index. Bibliography. A discussion of school and society, the internationalization of education, and research and innovations in education make up the first half of the book. The remainder is devoted to describing the future of education and some planning needs.

HUTCHINS, ROBERT M. *Learning Society.* New York: Frederick A. Praeger, 1968. 142 pages. Index. This book describes the circumstances of present-day education. Technology of education, liberal education, and the university are some of the topics covered. The author concludes the book with a plea that a learning society can and must be developed.

MACKENZIE, NORMA; POSTGATE, RICHMOND; and SCUPHAM, JOHN (eds.). *Open Learning.* Paris: Unesco Press, 1975. 498 pages. Bibliography. The first portion of this massive volume is devoted to describing some perspectives, problems, and practice in open learning. The remainder of the book describes case studies of open learning activities throughout the world. Nearly one-third of the book contains descriptions by Meierhenry and other American writers of special non-traditional programs in the United States.

MAYHEW, LEWIS B. *The Carnegie Commission on Higher Education.* San Franscisco: Jossey-Bass, 1973. 441 pages. Title and general indexes. This huge volume describes the higher education picture in the United States. Such issues as financing, training professionals, and future trends are covered.

MUSHKIN, SELMA J. (ed.). *Recurrent Education.* Washington, D.C.: National Institute of Education, U.S. Department of Health, Education, and Welfare, 1973. 347 pages. Index. Selective bibliography. This volume represents the work and findings of a conference that studied the recurrent education (lifelong learning) movement in Europe. Policy issues, specific programs, target groups, and financial considerations are some of the issues addressed.

TOFFLER, ALVIN (ed.). *Learning for Tomorrow.* New York: Random House, 1974. 421 pages. Index. Appendix. A variety of articles by various authors discuss the relationship of the future and education. The development of the individual, future curriculum needs, and resources for studying the future are also discussed.

TUBBS, WALTER E., JR. *Toward a Community of Seekers: A Report on Experimental Higher Education.* Lincoln, Nebr.: Nebraska Curriculum Development Center, University of Nebraska, 1972. 299 pages. Appendixes. Utilizing a symposium approach, the book reports on a variety of trends and innovations in higher education. Off-campus education, financing suggestions, and the higher education bill are also discussed. The appendixes contain descriptions of various innovative higher education approaches.

Suggested references in other chapters are as follows:

Chapter 1. Carnegie Commission on Higher Education   Chapter 3. Knowles
          Gould and Cross   *Perspectives* . . .
          Illich
          Ohlinger and McCarthy

* Cy Houle

Kidd

Paul Sheets

Paul Esser

Gratten

John W. Powell (1st philosopher)

A. A. Liberight

2596609 .